T0208156

THE Healthy LEADER

A Guide to Empowering Character in Ministry & Marketplace Leaders

Anna Michelle

WESTBOW
PRESS®
A DIVISION OF THOMAS NELSON
& ZONDERVAN

WestBow Press books may be ordered through booksellers or by contacting:

WestBow Press
A Division of Thomas Nelson & Zondervan
1663 Liberty Drive
Bloomington, IN 47403
www.westbowpress.com
1 (866) 928-1240

Scripture quotations are from the ESV® Bible (The Holy Bible, English Standard Version®), copyright © 2001 by Crossway, a publishing ministry of Good News Publishers. Used by permission. All rights reserved.

ISBN: 978-1-9736-3097-5 (sc)
ISBN: 978-1-9736-3096-8 (e)

Print information available on the last page.

WestBow Press rev. date: 06/26/2018

Contents

Dedication

To the people that challenged me the most

Jesus!! you are the love of my life. You taught me everything I know and set me free from bondage. You sacrificed your life for me and imparted your spirit within me. You allowed me to hear your still small voice, transformed my world, and taught me how to love people who weren't lovable.

My children. I fought for you, I cried for you, I nurtured you, and in return you had patience with me. You loved me, during the most difficult times. You've watched me grow more than anyone, and experienced the pains of my past failures. Because of you, we've survived the past; we're overcoming the present, and changing our future together.

To my parents, who loved me, sheltered me, taught me the value of hard work, prayed for me and instilled the love of Christ in me. I thank you!

To my sisters and brothers. You have been such an inspiration in my life. I thank God every day for sending people in my life whose heart is genuine and pure. No! You're not perfect, but you are all are special in your own way. Thank you for standing by me, challenging me and making sure I succeeded.

There were many others who traveled with me on my journey of change, and I'm forever grateful. Without the lessons I learned, from entering your paths, I would not be free enough to be me. Thank you!

About the author

Michelle Franklin is a woman of excellence. She's passionate about leadership and takes pride in developing herself and others. She walks with the wisdom of Abigail and is clothed with dignity and strength. Through her obedience to God, she learned the power of submission and commitment. In 2012 she was told by her leaders that, " the spirit of leadership is upon you to empower leaders of many nations". She's a mother of two, a sister, a daughter, an aunt and friend to many. Her mission is to train leaders in the Marketplace to uphold the code of ethics, professionalism and re-implement morals that influence the next generation. Throughout the years, she's committed herself to leadership and character development. Later she became a member of The John C Maxwell Team. She studied communications & psychology at South Suburban College, she's a License Christian Counselor and is currently pursuing her degree in biblical counseling.

In 2014 she was led to become a Certified Life Recovery Coach. With her gift, she plans to help leader's recover from a set back due to character deficiencies and mistakes from their past. She's the CEO of Lilies Miracle Care Foundation. An organization geared towards helping families and healthcare workers understand what matters most to those suffering illness or loss. She's the founder of CLS Reflection, an organization established to strengthen partnerships, character, leadership, and stewardship (financial stability). She's a Mentor, and Published Author of five books. If you haven't discovered who you are, she will motivate you to keep pushing until you find it. This book was written to encourage you to embrace your process to destiny, Enjoy!

Foreword
by John Veal

In her book "The Healthy Leader", Michelle Franklin takes us on an odyssey which heads into the direction of strong, effective leadership, inside the church and out. The author provides practical information and relevant strategies that will assist in preventing you from falling into the habits of poorly executed management. Franklin cleverly uses personal experiences to further illustrate a myriad of strong points throughout this book. The use of these stories helps to ingratiate the reader, making them feel her words instead of just reading them. She is very transparent regarding her trials and tribulations contained in the process of becoming a leader. In my opinion, the use of real-world connections further embeds what the author is trying to convey to her audience. This makes Franklin's manuscript more original and unlike any of its predecessors.

Her use of Scripture is generous. It's applied here as a means of providing biblical truths as a foundational base. Franklin shares a great deal of revelation about the sound teaching. It will cause you to re-examine your own leadership style. You will feel an urge to take a self-inventory of what's working and what's not. I love how she emphasizes the importance of character. The great sports figure, John Wooden, said, and I quote, "Ability or talent may get you the top, but it takes character to keep you there." It's quite evident that Michelle has learned this because this premise resounds within the pages of this manuscript.

Health is defined as the state of being free from illness or injury. In this season, we have many unhealthy or ill leaders in the world. This book has the potential to heal a lot of "sick" leaders, changing them into "healed" ones. Michelle Franklin carries a mantle or burden for leaders, especially those within the House of the Lord. I truly believe that her writing will provide a different perspective concerning the diversity of leadership and how it's effectively carried out. The reader will be equipped with strategies that will help them discover their own innate leadership styles, effectively bringing them to the surface. They will gain the capacity to lead from an "original" standpoint, not as a carbon copy of a great original. Creativity is paramount in developing strategies that will cause them to be effective and fit leaders! After "eating" of this book, you will gain the proper nutrition needed to complete your journey to becoming a healthy leader.

Introduction:
My process
(Rom 5:1-4)

Therefore, since we have been justified through faith, we have peace with God through our Lord Jesus Christ, through whom we have gained access by faith into this grace in which we now stand. And we boast in the hope of the glory of God. Not only so, but we also glory in our sufferings, because we know that suffering produces perseverance; perseverance, character; and character, hope, and hope does not put us to shame, because God's love has been poured out into our hearts through the Holy Spirit, who has been given to us.

In November of 2016, I decided to answer the prophetic call upon my life. I was excited and nervous at the same time. As I walked up to the altar to have hands laid on me, I instantly knew that my life would never be the same. While others were celebrating this joyous occasion, I was smiling yet quiet because I knew adversity was getting ready to hit me. I was growing into the woman God had predestined me to be; which means, I was stuck in transition. I had to be processed like everyone who answered the called. About 4 months before my affirmation service my home caught fire. Apparently, it was an electrical fire that started in the attic and had been burning for weeks. The fire department was shocked that my children and I made it out safely. In June 2017 I started suffering in my body due to a heart problem. Shortly afterward, I was told I needed immediate open-heart surgery. I was told that my right artery had grown in the wrong place; it was something that happened at birth. Obviously, I was a miracle. Doctors were blown away and questioned me over and over trying to figure out why I was still alive. Not long after that, I was being tested in my finances. I was losing everything in my life that I valued. After having major surgery, my uncle passed, my son's father was murdered, and my cousin passed away suddenly, all in a matter of five months. I was confused and disorientated. Everything I had worked so hard to accomplish seemed to be falling apart, and it felt like a great force was trying to take my life. However, I was determined to push myself to keep growing, and believing in God. I had to fight off fear, depression, anxiety, and anger. Although I was hurting, I understood that I still had responsibilities as a mother, daughter, sister, leader in church and my assignment. Everyone has always depended upon me to be strong and have all the answers. However, I had reached a point where I needed someone. With everything I was losing, my character soon came under great attack by people I knew and loved. I wanted to fight back but was instructed by God, to be still and quiet. It was through my faith in God that I was able to overcome the process and still keep my integrity. During my childhood, no one ever informed me that suffering helps to shape and create our life experiences, and our life experiences create longevity in our character. I live in a generation that wants to travel down an easy road and doesn't believe in hard work. Determination in the midst of adversity, that's what produced my character. Learning more about me, what I like, didn't like, my strengths and weaknesses were all revealed in my suffering. It was being tested in the fire that revealed my identity and shows me what I was capable of. My process taught me how to love people, and increased my desire to help them. Because I experienced so much pain, I didn't want anyone to suffer like me. So I set out to teach others how to avoid pitfalls caused by character defects. Nothing teaches you how to rebound from a fall like failure. Failure caused me to isolate myself, and isolation made me humble. Character is a matter of the heart, and through my process, God changed my heart.

(1 Sam 16:7) says

But the Lord said to Samuel, do not look on his appearance or on the height of his stature, because I have rejected him. For the Lord sees not as man sees; man looks on the outward appearance but the Lord looks on the heart.

Every character trait I've discovered within myself was produced in my struggle, and now the elements are deeply rooted in my heart & spirit. Love, joy, peace, forbearance kindness, goodness, faithfulness, gentleness, and self-control. I've never been this happy in my life, and to be honest, my priorities are now right. My footsteps are secure because I yielded to God, my process and the leaders He placed in my life. The Bible teaches us that good character is to be desired. It's what releases favor over our lives and bring us before great men. We were made in the image of God, which means we were created to function in the fullness of His character. Mercy, grace, integrity, commitment, compassion, submission, obedience, love, humility, and forgiveness are all apart of Christ character. Christ Character is the foundation, and His leadership provides structure to keep your gifts polished. That means the only thing that holds us together is the foundation of our character and our leadership capabilities. Without enduring hardship, my life could have turned out like Judas. Judas had flaws but was still usable. That's why we should never assume that being in a position of leadership and flowing in our gifts, exempts us from having unchecked flaws. His only problem was not getting free or finding balance. He wasn't teachable, which was why he set under the anointing, yet refused to grab hold of it. Each day I learn something new concerning myself. Why? Because as humans we are supposed to evolve and Flourish into someone better. My process shifted my perspective concerning the true meaning of character and leadership.

Shifting your perspective requires a change in your vision. Vision brings value to the world around us. Times and seasons will change, and we don't have control over it. That means we must shift our perspective to adjust to the seasons. We can't grow in life only living from past Perspectives. We must always see things as they relate to what's happening now and what they have the power to become. This is the only way to bring forth transformation. Our perspective is a matter of our perception. The way we see things in our mind. If we can see it in our mind, it can become tangible in our natural. Visionary leaders are leaders who focus on bringing tangible manifestations for present and future existence. They understand the power of release. Leadership helps to shift the vision of people, which is true servanthood. Servanthood cannot be effective until you learn to deny yourself. Denying yourself will help keep things in proper perspective when serving. As leaders it's easy to fall victim to the spirit of pride and think that leadership is about recruiting followers. True leadership is about helping others to fly out of their nest. Several things are required to shift in order to bring change. That is, your vision, thinking, hearing, heart, and your environment.

Our senses and our environment play a major role in our advancement. If our senses are not governed by the right influence, we could conform to a false image instead of transforming into God's divine image. Conform means to behave based on socially acceptable standards. It means you follow the crowd as if you have no mind of your own. To transform it means to change in character, structure, appearance and to undergo a change in your heart, which is what changes perception. The reason we must focus on transformation is because of our ability to lead. Leaders refuse to conform to what's socially popular and believes in the growth and development of their team. Their focus is to shift their senses. Teaching them to understand the power of what they speak, the importance of guarding their hearing, restoring their vision so they can see, and influencing the heart and mind to be open to what we can become. Leading your team to victory starts, with developing their character first.

Everyone can lead and will be given a measure. Staying in your measure will help you lead by example with your team. Sometimes we think that as leader's people need us and we don't need them. But, the reality is this, without people following us, we cannot lead, and people must choose to follow. Leaders are change agents who honor people, not just leaders in a position of authority, but all men. We are gifted to help gifted people, and the only way to draw from what's on the inside of people you must show honor. When you honor people, you will never have to beg or pressure them to do anything. People will come into an agreement even when they don't see what you see. They will still buy into you and your vision.

2 Kings 6:17 says,

Then Elisha prayed and said, "O LORD, please open his eyes that he may see." So the LORD opened the eyes of the young man, and he saw, and behold, the mountain was full of horses and chariots of fire all around Elisha.

Elisha never got mad because he couldn't see, neither did the man stop following. Leaders that want to be effective will restore the vision of their team. They will encourage those who don't have it and won't be intimidated by those who do. Never allow yourself to think you know more than every member of your team if you know more than everyone on your team you will never bring in a sustainable increase.

It doesn't matter where the wisdom comes from, as long as you understand it. Your interactions with all people will determine whether you will be effective in the marketplace. So, don't shut down people because they're not on your level. Whatever kind of leader you are you must serve people, including those who haven't reach the full age of maturity. Serving the earth is a never-ending process, and it creates humility. Servanthood was never intended to replace our gifts but to enhance them. Serving people doesn't mean we're developed in our character and without getting developed; we will never walk in the fullness of our purpose. Character and leadership development are important, and we should invest more of our time into growing in those areas. When we grow in character and leadership, we transform like a flower that blooms.

Transformational leaders focus is to change the mind and stabilize their teams. They challenge you to take ownership of your life through tasks that will enhance your day-to-day performance. Transformation is a renewing. You are taught to set structure, standards, and goals that will advance your life. Our world is shaped and formed based on what we have been taught to believe. We became what people wanted us to become or what's needed in our society. Which means we conform more than we lead. When leaders conform instead of transforming, they find it hard to assume responsibility for their actions. Whether right or wrong, when you are a leader assuming responsibility is a must. It's something that comes from the heart. It's easy to blame someone else when you've conformed to him or her. God predetermined your role as a leader, but the making process determines whether or not you're ready to fulfill it.

Today, our responses are usually based on first impressions. The way others look, carry themselves, who they hang around and the way they live. Good leadership is building a relationship with your team with a clear perception of them. It's being able to perceive like Adam so that you can effectively speak into their lives. It's not allowing your opinion and the opinions of others to define them. Sometimes understanding core and secondary beliefs are important when leading. When you don't understand a person's background or environment, you'll hold them back and won't trust them. Do we have time to evaluate everyone on our team? Yes! Understanding their culture helps us not to pass judgment when things are not done our way. We all are different and accomplish tasks differently.

As humans, our core belief takes on a greater role. When a parent teaches a child to hate based on race or gender, we should never follow that person. The root of the stronghold within them is deep and needs to be destroyed. Secondary beliefs are when one is being influenced by the world around them. They also have strongholds, but they're not as deeply rooted. They are seen on the surface and can be detected immediately. Whether we want to believe it our culture has a huge effect on our character, the way we lead, follow and how we treat people. There are certain tasks that some people can't do. Does it mean they can't follow instructions, no! It simply means they're not equipped for that assignment. No one applies for a position unless they have training. Building a relationship with your team will help you understand what task to give each person. Therefore, we should never give individuals assignments without proper training and evaluation. Elevations should only come after evaluation. Start your journey by enhancing your leadership abilities. The process will help you understand your role and the potential of the people you're training. If I could leave you with one piece of advice, it would be to embrace the art of listening. A person with good character is slow to speak, and swift to hear, so their words can be established to cancel out misunderstandings, within the confines of your team. I was called into the office. But, the making process developed my character.

Character & Leadership

Developing your character will unlock the leader within you and stabilize your gifts. Sometimes we place people where we think they should go. However, the purpose of leadership is leading them into their purpose. Yes, everyone wants to operate in his or her gift, but if we learn to develop character first, leadership second, then the gift, we would see far greater results. During the character building process, you will discover the leader within you first. The next thing that's revealed is your gifts. Most of us become so excited about the gifts that we move out and walk in them before being fully developed as a leader. The gifts are only the vehicles used to transport us to our purpose, which is our destination. When a person doesn't submit to the character building process, it causes them to rely on a weak gift. The gift becomes weak when the character isn't strong, and the leader in them hasn't been developed. When God speaks to us, He speaks in parts, giving us a piece of His puzzle. That means we must put things into proper alignment, and only the leader in you can do that.

Organization is a skill we usually learn in stage two (leadership building); following instruction is learned in stage one. Our character building stage will give a positive outlook on life. It will help you build confidence, integrity, commitment and most of all awareness of your strengths and weaknesses. Many people do not like to go through a transformation because they lack endurance. Endurance is something that's discovered during the character stage and strengthened during leadership training. When you discover your level of endurance, it makes it a lot easier to endure as a leader. The process is designed to help you build through hardship, the place where character flaws are torn down, and character traits are resurrected. Professionalism is a matter of character. Often we go through life encountering leaders who are not professional. This is always a result of character deficiencies. Character deficiencies are just unchecked flaws. We all have them, but the key is finding your balance. Strong leaders are professional leaders. Let's examine professionalism a little closer.

Characteristics for professionalism

Core value of Appearance

The law of appearance is when you understand that presentation is everything. Whether you are dressing for an assignment, speaking in front of a crowd, going to school, church or just an outing, your appearance will attract attention. The attention it attracts will be sorely up to you. We must understand who and what system we are representing. The first person we work on is ourselves. Loving ourselves and building self- confidence will express our worth to others. Looking good always let them know how much we value ourselves and will prevent negative assumptions from being made.

Often, our appearance is used to cover up hidden things about us. Even when we look the part, our appearance can send an impression that everything is ok, when we want to go home and die. People with a nasty attitude and disposition are always unprofessional, mean, and rude and no matter what their outward appearance looks like, all we'll ever see is their dysfunction. We are living in a time when personal image is everything. Everyone wants to brand him or herself. But branding is not always the real you. To succeed we're told to create an image that everyone wants.

We become what others expect us to become. But we were created to be authentic, as leaders and authentic in our gifts. Without the authenticity of our gift and character the world cannot exist and grow beyond its currency. The law of appearance is when you allow people to see your character through your facial expression, body language, your speech, the way you dress and using it to make up your image. I always tell people there are certain platforms they will never grace when they don't dress the part. You must dress for greatness, but be free enough for it to be a reality!

Body language is one of the most dangerous because it's communicated. This form of communication allows people to see where you are in your emotions, physically and mentally. When you're not feeling your best, it will show up in your body language. When you're prideful if will show up in your body language and when your body is riddled with pain, it will always show up. While working at a hospital, I would often see people come in who were sick and angry. Because of their sickness and a lack of support some experienced, it was seen in their body language. Body language is used in every area of our lives especially in our ability to lead. When a person has an unteachable spirit, it will be shown in their body language. That's why we must work on this area while we're going through the character building stage. Non-verbal skills can be developed, and they will also tell others when your intimidated, lazy, immature, confidence and friendly. It lets others know that you understand the power and authority you have been given, and you know what to do what it. I remember growing up and my mother giving us a look that signaled to us she meant business. We knew when to shut up and when we were in trouble. If your body language is off, it will interfere with your ability to gain the influence you're looking for as a leader.

Core value of Manners

If there's one thing missing in our society, it's people with manners. Manners were usually taught to us growing up. Our parents, teachers and those responsible for us checked behavior, our conduct, demeanor, and attitude. Developing a habit of being nice to others, being considerate and treating others the way you want to be treated is a way of showing good manners. Leaders with good manners and morals lead more effectively than others. Their capacity to have more will always be increased because God can trust them with His children.

Core value of sociable

Being sociable is required for every person who desires a position of leadership. Throughout most of my years as an adult I've seem leaders on my job, and ministers in my church get up to speak, but when they came down they were not approachable. They lack the ability to build solid, firm, and stable relationships. This often is brought on by trauma that occurred from their past. People who exhibit these symptoms are usually known as being nonchalant.

Nonchalant is when a person tries to avoid pain or major life event (not always pain) by putting up defense mechanisms that might affect their emotions/self-esteem. An example would be when I asked a friend if she desired to be married, she acted as if she didn't care about getting married. Believing she was called to be single was her way of coping with her being 50, never been married and hadn't dated in the past ten years. Sometimes peoples fear of not accomplishing their desires become so strong that walls are placed up, as a way of protecting their heart from being broken in an event it doesn't happen. Leaders who've developed this trait are unsure about their journey and won't be able to articulate the vision with clarity. They'll be afraid to trust their team, and won't be able to effectively communicate with them.

Core value of strong-willed

Being strong-willed is a character flaw and positive trait. It comes from the root of pride, rejection and a need to always have your way. It's best seen in children and should be corrected immediately. Because it carries a positive meaning, you may not have to stop being strong-willed all you need is balance. Strong-willed individuals would likely accomplish their goals because they're fueled by passion and momentum. However, without balance leaders who battle with this spirit can become controlling, stubborn, prideful and operate in manipulation to get followers.

Core value of forgiveness

Without forgiveness, you will never move forward into your destiny. Forgiveness is the key to unlocking another level of influence. People places and things that wouldn't normally be available to you would be released to you. Forgiveness is the action or process of forgiving or being forgiven. The reason a lot of leaders have failed is due to harboring un-forgiveness in their heart. There is a saying that people in church use when referring to why many have left the church. It's called church hurt. But church hurt is nothing more than people hurt. As humans, we hurt each other; we have disagreements and get offended. If we hold on to what others have done to us depression comes in, so does sickness. In January 2016 I experienced a betrayal I never thought I would ever experience. My name was run through the mud because I wouldn't allow a former friend to manipulate me. As much as I wanted to hate her, I couldn't. I knew that receiving my blessing was based on me being free enough to pursue them. God wants to bless us, but He can't get it to us when we have un-forgiveness. Un-forgiveness feels like a weight pressing down on us. As long as the weight is there, we cannot be open to receive anything else.

Core value of professionalism

Professionalism is a key, but missing ingredients in our organization and ministries. The reason many leaders' struggle in this area is because we have become a nation centered on, money. People are looking for quick ways to grow their revenue. Professionalism makes up a set of different attributes like accountability, competency, honesty and common sense. One day I was on the phone with a friend frustrated at her son for pouring grease down the sink. She yelled "where is his common sense", I replied, "one thing about common sense is that it's not so common." Everyone doesn't inherit that trait. However, common sense is something that can be developed. Leaders who encompass professionalism are reliable and walk with the utmost integrity one could have. They don't tell half true's, backbit, stir up confusion, or manipulate others to get ahead. For years, I've seen political figures lack professionalism when trying to win a race. If the next generation of leaders doesn't work to perfect their character and embody this trait the systems will continue to crash. My advice would be to make a personal commitment to improve your skills, competency, and expertise character and leadership skills.

Core value of Creativity

The law of creativity speaks to the authentic. Those that embrace this law understand the power of creating good thought habits that bring manifestation to the world around them. They are visionary and builders in heart and spirit. The reason I've chosen creativity as a law is because we all were born with the ability to create. Creativity is one of the characteristics that God instilled in every one of us. In recent years, we have been taught to follow the creativity of others. However, leaders will never get the full benefits of their teams if they don't allow them to explore the creativity of their minds.

We must put a demand on others and ourselves to come up higher for the next generation. First, it was information and today its technology, but what will we be embarking upon next. If we're going to shape the next move, we must seek our creator for a concept that will generate new ideas for all the systems of the world. Although we should embrace self-love and worth we should never get to a place when we stop relying on the mind of the great I AM to lead us. On the day of Pentecost God released His spirit upon all flesh and gave insight into mankind about His creation and its ability to influence other nations. Because His hand is on us, He influences our perception. Again, perception is a matter of the mind that creates mental images and establishes our imagination. When we meditate on our imagination, we have the power to become it. Leaders who embrace this law will leave a legacy not just to their circle but also to the world.

Core value of Prudence

The law of prudence is your ability to see ahead. It's governing and disciplining you by use of reasoning. When people look at you, do they see a prudence spirit or do they see someone who is judgmental or someone controlled by their emotion and assumptions. Are you a person who looks for the truth and process all source of information given to you? If so you might have a prudence spirit. To be effective in your gifts or any assignment you have it's going to require you to walk in wisdom, insight, and knowledge. If leaders can't see ahead, they can't get ahead. The lack of a prudence spirit will soon become evident to your followers, and when it does, you'll lose!

Core value of Curiosity

Curiosity is the trait that has shaped our world, and a lack of it is destroying it. As I set in the ER one hot summer infused with pain, I was disappointed at the lack of compassion and understanding I was receiving from the staff. I kept telling myself if I could just get to the back and see the doctors I know they will help. Little did I know the doctors had no interest in finding out what was wrong with me? They were only there to help me cope with the pain, not to find out why it was invading my body. I was angry yet furious. Needless to say, while I lay in the bed crying, it hit me. Doctors have become so driven by money, that they've lost their curiosity. Curiosity is very rare today.

Curiosity means you have a strong desire to learn or know why something is occurring. People use to become doctors and Scientist because they wanted to cure people, not manages their care. When people were sick, or devastation hit our lands they wanted to know why and find a solution to stop it. Curiosity creates a monument that keeps you in hot pursuit of your goals. What the world needs today more than ever, are problem solvers. We're taught to call the police when there is a problem. But, most Police officers are only trained to search for a suspect in a crime. However, A suspect is just an idea or impression of someone or something. It isn't proof of their guilt. Because they're not taught to embrace the gift of curiosity, it's easy for them to lead according to hearsay and assumptions.

It always takes a curious person to solve a crime and bring justice to a victim's family. If the spirit of curiosity led our judicial system, we'd have less false convictions. I once heard a statement on Law & Order "prosecutors get convictions, but great prosecutors get justice". You can convict anyone of a crime, but justice is only served when you convict the right person of the crime. A statement I live by today is, "The greatest problem solvers are those who were curious enough to search for the solution". Leader's who plan to go far and leave a lasting legacy will unlock the gift of curiosity within them.

Changing yourself matters most

Self- empowerment

Self -empowerment is empowering yourself before you consider empowering others. If you don't believe in yourself how can you encourage others, that they'll achieve theirs? Now the law of self- empowerment is when you discover your strengths, your weaknesses, and flaws. Discovering them will help you strategize and implement a plan of transition. Transitioning from a place of powerlessness to wholeness, where one finds their inner- peace. Once you've become whole leading others will become inevitable. The world is always looking for self – help books to help them understand who they are and why they were created. That's why we have leaders. But, leaders must be made, and during the making process is when we learn to empower others and ourselves. Empowerment is an inner strength that others will recognize and use to define our character and determine whether or not they'll follow our lead.

Self- discipline

We can always develop a system for our values principles and morals. But the integrity of our character comes from a crucified will that's in alignment with our purpose. Self-discipline is a decision to lay aside desires that will stop you from upholding the values and principles you've once committed to. Self- discipline is best in our actions through the time of hardship, disappointments, and adversity. We will never fulfill our purpose without consistency, and consistency is a strength that's built up when we set out to self- discipline ourselves. Every storm that came to destroy me was an opportunity to express my character. Weather good or bad. I recognized how my response to every negative situation and person was not only different but became better. It resulted from a disciplined life of reading, meditating, self-discovery and praying. As you submit to learning more about yourself truth will always be revealed. Discipline will help to improve you as a leader and let others know they can rely on you.

Self- critical

This weighs on me the most. Growing up it seems as if I failed at everything. So, when I became a grown woman, I became very critical of myself. No one had to tell me I was wrong, I just knew. Whatever the problem was I was the blame. I didn't like the way I looked on the outside or the inside. Every time I looked in the mirror I was fat, ugly and the girl no one wanted. This mentality followed me until I searched out the leader within me. In order to be the leader I was destined to be, I had to embrace me. All of me!

13

I had to love me and approve of me before asking others to accept me. When a leader is always critical of themselves, it makes it easy to be critical of others. Being critical of others means you have a judgmental spirit, and no one wants to follow someone who's always judgmental of them. Leaders who show this weakness will find it hard to get others to respect them. People will follow you because your heart towards them is pure, but they will find it hard to show you the respect leaders should have. What am I saying, people will overstep their boundaries with you. They may respect you, but not your position of authority. I challenge you to love and accept yourself first. When you do, you'll become a better leader.

Self-sufficient

Due to my low-esteem, believing no one wanted me, I become self-sufficient. Now, being self- sufficient starts in the mind. I remember telling myself as a child, we I get older; I will never rely on anyone to help me with anything. I became an independent woman, as we like to call it. However, it didn't last long. The more I tried to believe I didn't need anyone, the more I failed. I became confident in the materials I acquired, yet, inside I still felt needy and continued to find myself broken and broke. God had to break me down till I had nothing. I would often talk about those on public assistance, declaring that I would never need it. But to my surprise, I hit rock bottom, and there I was standing in the line, looking for help. Being self- sufficient isn't a bad thing, but can become one. It can start in the mind when you're a child. If everyone in the world were self- sufficient we wouldn't have a need for the governmental assistance, so becoming self- sufficient is the goal. However, you should never allow your position of not needing support make you become so prideful, that you don't ask for help when you need it. Neither should you display a lack of compassion on those who are experiencing hard times. Leadership is self-sufficient and helps those who are not sufficiently capable of taking care of themselves.

Self- conscious

What can I say? I had issues. But my freedom is now an opportunity to free others. In 1999 I had a breast reduction. Why? I was self-conscious about everything. My big breast made me feel like everyone was watching me. I felt like the girl from the movie Carrie, who cried "they're all going to look at me". Every decision I made to change my appearance was due to low-esteem and fear. That's right fear. Being self-conscious comes from the spirit of fear being rooted within you. I was so bound I thought getting smaller breast would make me feel and look better. But, when I had surgery, I wasn't pleased. After having the surgery people now saw my stomach. No matter how hard I fought to change the outward appearance, it was never enough. I was hurting on the inside, and until I broke free from that, I would be self- conscious about everything. Leaders who're self-conscious will deal with the spirit of rejection. They will always think others are talking about them, don't like what they're wearing, or just don't like them. These types of leaders lead from their position because of their inability to build effective relationships, because of their lack of trust.

Self- denying

Self- denying is a form of self- discipline. It's done to sacrifice one's desires for a greater cause (the needs of others). It's an unselfish act. This helped to identify me as a leader. Discipline prepared me for my assignment, but denying myself brought fourth humility. As a leader, I realized that I couldn't just prepare for the assignment to lead others into their destiny if I wasn't willing to put their needs ahead of my own. I knew my time to enjoy my personal pleasures were coming. Loving others and helping them reach their full potential is my passion and denying myself was easy. Disciplining myself was what I hated. But it prepared me to deny myself.

The component of loyalty

One of the most important components required to build character & function in leadership is loyalty. Loyalty is the component that keeps your team following and builds self- confidence. It's the very thing that validates who you are, and whether or not you're trustworthy. Loyalty will always uncover hidden traits. Traits like, honesty, commitment, humility, and consistency; just to name a few. When there is no loyalty on your team, losing every battle then becomes inevitable. To win the war, your team must be secure and solid. That means, having a made-up mind about the leaders they've chosen to follow, and willing to make the necessary changes to follow the vision. Loyalty gives you, and your team vision, and fresh ideas that allows you to collaborate to overcome some of the toughest battles you'll ever face in life.

Loyalty cannot be bought, forced, or given to you based on delegated authority. It's something you must build through your relationships. That's one reason why building strong relationships is important. Often, we try to force loyalty upon people. I've heard leaders say, if you trust me, you're supposed to trust my team. However, it is based on my opinion and experience that, people will never trust people they haven't bought into; because buying into them requires us to establish our own relationships. We can follow delegated authority but have no real loyalty to them. How can I trust you, when I don't know you? We expect people to ride off the influence of the leader, and in today's society that's just impossible. There were times I was held back from elevated positions, or just being involved in assignments without an explanation. It wasn't until years later that I was told why. Apparently, delegated authority told the leader something false concerning me. Because the leader trusted their teams to the highest degree (not leaving room for error), they went along without validating that information. If someone on your team has unbalanced flaws and becomes intimidated by a newcomer, get ready for your building to collapse. I remember praying to the Lord, when He informed me, that my loyalty should never side with unrighteous behavior. When a member of your team tells you anything that could potentially damage your view of another always validate the information, before making any decisions concerning that person. After you collect all the information needed, your next step would be to call a meeting with all parties involved. You're building a team that will help you bring your vision to pass, so it's important to take every form of precaution to keep out bitterness, intimidation, offenses, and envy. The only way to keep unity is through loyalty. Now, let's evaluate misplace loyalty. Misplaced loyalty comes into your camp when there is a lack of intimacy. Intimacy basically knows a person's character through your relationship with them. Without building relationships, misplaced loyalty begins to form.

What does it mean when something has been misplaced? It means it has been incorrectly positioned or temporarily lost. It also means to be misled. Basically misguided. Therefore, when a person demonstrates misplace loyalty, it's when their loyalty is residing in a system or person they shouldn't be loyal to. Example: if you're a teller at a bank, and two of your friends come into the bank and rob it. Where should your loyal reside. At least 80% of America would say, with your friends. But true loyalty never sides with unrighteous behavior. Never! If your friends had any loyalty to you, they would've respected your job by not coming in to rob it. Your life and reputation will be put on the line because of the company you choose to keep. When they ask if anyone was able to recognize the criminals that rob the bank. If you say no, and they find out you do, your character, job, and life will

Four causes of unprofessional behavior!

Thesaurus & Wikipedia definition

Uncooperative – stubborn, stiff-necked, unyielding, difficult disobedient. Someone unwilling to cooperate and unsupportive of your vision. Leaders need people who're going to be cooperative with the vision.

Unappreciative- no understanding, not able to recognize or value someone. It also refers to someone who's ungrateful, heartless and careless. Leaders need to be appreciated and must appreciate others. This will increase the momentum within your team.

Unstable- unstable means you're double-minded, disturbed, confuse, and prone to psychiatric problems. As the dictionary puts it. It's recognized with people who've experienced sudden changes in their mood, unbalanced and unsound mentally. Leaders are builder, and they need people who are stable enough to help them finish the work of the vision.

Unpolished- unfinished, uncultivated, and unrefined in style and behavior. Leaders must always take pride in how they look and display the spirit of excellence in everything they do.

A person of good character and leadership should always watch out for people who will try and pervert their will to do what's right. Great leaders will cooperate with the vision, appreciate their team, and they're stable. Their skills, character, and appearance all have been polished in excellence.

Character

Character development <u>*Webster definition*</u> – as mental and moral qualities distinctive to an individual. It's made up of personality nature disposition temperament temper mentality, make-up and the ethical value of a human. It's what distinguishes us from one another and makes us individuals.

There are many qualities and components that define a person of good character. Integrity, trustworthy, compassionate, great humanitarian, good spirit, good intentions, stable, secure firm unwavering, enduring, reliable, noble, honorable, reputable, upright, unselfish, and generous. Courage, empathy, honesty, and loyalty are also a few. If a person lacks in one characteristic it doesn't mean they don't have good character. What makes a person of good character is when they have a teachable spirit. A person with a teachable spirit is someone who understands the value of leadership. They operate in obedience integrity and humility, absent of pride.

As humans, we mess-up and say things we don't mean. If we define everyone's character by every mess up or things we do in the heat of the moment, we will always fail and judge everyone every moment of the day. Developing good character means always leaving room for growth. A lot of times we think if we are great in our gifts and talents we're ready for the big world and a position of leadership. So, we fight and work hard to perfect our craft. However, you will never be effective in your gift until you learn to bring stabilization to your character and learn about your leadership capabilities.

Character development is first; leadership development is next, then starts the training in your gift. When you follow these steps in that order, and the door of opportunity opens, you'll be ready. There are many distinguishing characteristics that we have, and you should never expect everyone to have the same ones you have although it's possible. Character deficiencies usually occur when we don't have balance in our traits and when we're not working on our flaws. Certain traits and flaws are developed in childhood years and go unnoticed. I've even seen where children could be disrespectful, and it was taped and aired on social media for laughter. When we fail to grow our children up to have good character, we open the door for a jobless, murderous, evil and poverty generation. Through character, we create reputations that can be trusted. Marriages aren't working because people are building on false pretense. Everyone wants wealth and will stop at nothing till they get what they want. Women and men have put their happiness, family and even their beliefs to the side just to connect with someone who has money.

Don't get me wrong I want to be wealthy, but my assignment to impact this nation with my gift is greater. Sometimes we get so focused on wealth we stop creating balance in the one thing that's going to sustain us, which is our character. Chasing after wealth is why some people inherit a bad reputation. If we allow our purpose to be greater than our desire to be rich, we'll take time to establish our character. Self- discovery is a stage we often re-visit. When we are babes, we gravitate to people and objects trying to discover the purpose of everything. But when we enter the adolescence stages, we struggle.

This stage is the most important stage of our lives because they are the developmental stages. It's a time when humans are developed socially, emotional, physical and cognitive. This is also the stage that shapes our character and the stage that make the most impact on our lives. Surrounded by mood swings and strange behavior teens develop their own mindset and viewpoint before adulthood. Although they are teens, we must remember, everything that happens in that stage has the potential to destroy their reputation and possibly their future. Because of the trauma that many of us go through, we lose sight of some of our passions and uniqueness. With our intent to cover and block the difficult times we've experienced we lose our momentum to pursue what we believed our purpose is. Therefore, when we get older and find ourselves on a road of self-discovery God has to unlock certain gifts and characteristics that were bury. It's also a time of revealing flaws that hindered us from producing. Flaws are typically formed during the adolescence stages. Through our willingness to believe that the child will grow out of the flawed and negative behavior, we overlook certain flaws instead of correcting them. Correction means that something was done wrong and we must show each other how to do it right. People who exhibit a lot of character deficiencies usually develop unteachable spirit over time.

If we bring more correction at this stage, we'll have more leaders with good character for the next generation. Take a moment to go over this list of words to identify your strength and weaknesses.

Peculiar	Energetic	Kind	Considerate
Enthusiasm	Joyful	Meek	Good-humored
Adventurous	Compassionate	Creativity	Good - listener
Generous	Dependability	High – spirited	Charming

Overcautious	Indecisive	Short- tempered	Shallow
Self- conscious	Vain	Timid	Passive
Absent- minded	Overly critical	Withdrawn	Sarcastic
Loud/Noisy	Unsociable	Opinionated	Arrogance

Now that you've taken your personal inventory check think about what type of reputation you've created for yourself with these characteristics. This can also be done by asking others, family, friends, and coworkers. Often, we judge others based on the contents of what we believe our character is. Our standards, what's best for us, what works for us and how we think. But our character separates us from one another. Everyone may not have the same character traits and qualities. Remember character distinguishes us from one another. Just because I don't have the same character traits that define you, doesn't mean I'm a bad person. It simply means I'm unique and different in my own way. Our individuality helps to shape our world. One man can't do it alone, which is why we need people. People who don't have what we have or able to can see what we see.

Joseph was a man of noble character. That means he was a man of good reputation well known, distinguished and a good renowned person. He did not want to embarrass Mary when he found out that she was with child, so he wanted to hide her. Hiding her from the world would have protected her from the negative energy coming from others. It was his character that wouldn't allow him to shame her. No one had to tell him to protect her, protecting her was just who he was. Even though he wasn't the father of Jesus (Mary son), he was willing to cover, protect and raise someone else's seed. This is the reputation everyone should aim for, a reputation of compassion and willingness to serve in any capacity. He was the definition of a real man and chosen for greatness because of his character. Even though there isn't much about his life's process, his character speaks loudly in the short verses we were given.

Leaders are responsible: Joseph was a man of good character, upright blameless, righteous, and a man who would conform to God's laws. He was called and chosen by God to protect Mary and cover the promise. God trusted him and gave him the warnings and instructions on when and where to relocate. He was a man of faith. (*Matt 1:19*)

Reputation

There are so many leaders with good reputations but not a good character. We can't continue to elevate people into a position, on the opinions of others. We must look for the quality of their character. Yes! We must have a good reputation. However, because it's only the opinion of others, we should seek to build relationships to learn their true character. People fake it 'till they make it daily. Every relationship takes time, understanding, and patience to build. Unfortunately for many, it cost too much to get to know the real person. Especially since many have become comfortable embracing the representatives. Getting to know people sometimes seems to be a waste of time to many. I like to say, *"A man's action produces the reputation that creates his character"*. God wants us to have a reputation that represents Him. The bible says do not let your good be evil spoken of, and our reputation could reflect that.

People, places, and things have the power to influence our character. Whenever you hang around people that are liars, up to no good, steal, cause division, backbite, or keep up confusion, you label yourself. Places we like to go. Clubs or even gyms will define us. For example, I never joined a gym that's filled with young people. I always join community centers because it's less confusion in the locker room. Because of that, I've built a reputation of being old.

Reputation is the opinions that others have of you, and it can be false. *"A man of good character will develop a good reputation". Matthew 16 says.* Jesus asks the disciples who do men say I am. Basically, He was asking them what was His reputation among the people. His leaders were His representatives and often spoke on His behalf, which was why He asked them what people thought about Him. If you want to know your reputation, it's best to ask your team. Jesus produced a reputation of good character, by establishing a relationship with His team, and His team was able to validate it. Let's examine closely how much we rely on reputation.

- We date people based on reputation and not character!

- We vote on reputation and not character.
- We hire on reputation and not character
- We elevate based on reputation and not character.
- We support celebrities based on reputation and not character.
- We support speakers based on reputation and not character.
- We support Doctors, lawyers, etc. based solely on reputation and not their character.
- We follow based on reputation and not character

Reputation can and will be manipulated by others. When others try and destroy you, they will send false information to others. That's why you must be in control of what and whom you allow in your circle. Even when they try and crucify your reputation they can't assassinate your character, only you can. Again, your character should build your reputation. Never ever allow your reputation to be in control. Allowing your reputation to define your character mean's you're conforming to what others called you when God called you to be an original. When you have a bad reputation, it tells people you cannot be trusted and will be expected to prove yourself. So do not be offended when they ask you to prove your loyalty and commitment. If they're willing to stick around it means they're not conforming to other's assumptions of you.

"Character is what we know, reputation is what we have heard." John C Maxwell

When Paul was on the road to Damascus, God not only changed his vision, He rebuilt his reputation. When his character changed, his name changed, and his reputation among the saints changed. (Acts 9:17)

- His vision changed.
- His mind- thinking (Reminder: change to way of thinking)
- His speech changed.
- His name changed.
- His character changed.
- His reputation changed.

If your reputation has become damaged, it's important that you step back, evaluate yourself and your circle. Doing this will help you determine what steps to take to repair it. Sometimes we develop a negative reputation because others have misinterpreted what we've said. Being misunderstood is a natural human experience. It's something we all go through, which is why you must be careful what you say when you say it and whom you say it to. People will try and ruin you because they can't control you, so a bad reputation (among some) may not always be your fault. However, when your character has been damaged, it will take a process to rebuild it. First, realize that people will always make their own assumption about you. Next, take time to collect and separate what's true and false. Then, you must find the source of the lie. Don't be defensive when you hear their opinions, just try and take control of what was said and use it for your advantage to bring clarity. Denounce any accusations as lies, clarify any misunderstandings and learn to speak up for yourself. Please try not to be rude, when doing so.

Being rude is a character flaw. Leaders will develop a negative reputation when they appear to be rude. A lot of times they will seem rude when there is a lack of understanding and negative perception coming from the other person. That's why everyone in leadership should be developed. Develop also means to be delivered. Character building should be a part of every school from every age. Our character gets stronger as we grow through the years, especially when we submit to the process. Everyone has a different process, and although I was delivered from smoking in one day, I still had to go through a process to keep deliverance in my mind. Some people enter the process stage and stop along the way. When you don't know who you are or your purpose it will affect your character, change your life and delay manifestations. Your process will teach you how to balance your character and adjust your body language so you won't seem rude to others. Personal development should be set as a goal we must accomplish.

Setting goals requires us to manage our time. Accomplishing them requires a process. Processing our time and re-arranging our lives will create balance to achieve our goals. When you set your goal to self- development you must first become familiar with your character traits and flaws. Success comes from knowing who you are and pursuing what you want to become. Never worry about your reputation, just work on your character and try seeing yourself for who you can become. Your character will speak for itself and create the reputation you're looking for. Never define yourself or others by flaws. To understand a person's unique strengths, we should find out what style or trait differs from our own. This is how we build strong, solid relationships. Our character should be excellent in and outside of the church.

1 Tim 3:7

And he must have a good reputation with those outside the church.

Now let's look at Character Flaws

Thesaurus & Wikipedia definition, online version

A character flaw is a limitation and imperfection problem. It affects the personality, actions, and abilities. It can also affect a person's motives and social interactions.

- A <u>minor flaw</u> is an imperfection, which distinguishes the character in the minds of others.
- A <u>major flaw</u> is a much more noticeable flaw that will bring hindrance and impairs the individual.
- A <u>tragic flaw</u> is Hamartia meaning missing the mark. The Greek words are translated sin. It is a flaw that causes a noble or exceptional character to bring about his own downfall and eventual his or her own death. An example will be misplaced trust, excessive curiosity, pride, and lack of self-control.

Things that cause a tragic flaw.

- Deliberate error
- Enviousness
- Defensiveness
- Entitlement
- Unreliable character

- Eagerness to please
- Sarcasm
- Jealousy
- Stubbornness
- Arrogance
- Perfectionist

A perfectionist is a character trait and flaw. Often, we try so hard to be great we become rude and disrespectful. We'll misuse our help, run over people, manipulate people and even harm them. Growing up I'd watch sports and how competitive the games were. I remember thinking, is winning everything. Your desire to be perfect will always become a cancer to your opponent. We weren't created to be perfect, but great in our own unique way. A perfectionist doesn't need to stop being excellent. They should learn to motivate themselves to just do their part and be great in their own measure even if it means not always being at the top level. They can learn to change their perception about accomplishing certain goals. They can learn their flaws and improve them. A perfectionist is often destroyed because their fears of not reaching their goals control them.

As I write, one person comes to mind, and that's Tonya Harding. Tonya Harding was a star athlete for the Winter Olympics and involved in a scandal surrounding another athlete. Although Harding denies having any involvement in the injury of her opponent, she pleaded guilty to conspiring to hinder the prosecution. She later was banned from the Olympics altogether. Hardings, and those around her, desires to be a perfectionist produced a desire to win at any cost even if it meant harming someone.

She was great in her own way. Now, I was young when all this transpired, but I remembered her story. However, I could only remember her downfall, not her success. When you fight to be perfect, you'll risk losing your integrity, more opportunities, and even your life.

A perfectionist doesn't understand the value of a process. When Jesus told the disciples this kind only come out through fasting and praying (Mark 9:29). He was implying that some goals are accomplished through a process. Your process will reveal the areas you need improvements in so you can become better. Whatever you are assigned to do will only prosper through your character. Awareness and balance will prevent unnecessary character flaws from taking over. I want to encourage you to be great, but not to allow your willingness to be perfect to damage you. Take a note of this flaw, and create the balance you need to perfect it.

Now, let look at territorial.
Territorial is a character flaw and a character trait

Territorial <u>Webster online defines it as</u> – ownership of an area or a land that relates to a territory.

Being territorial is a character flaw that can cause much damage to your team. A person said to be territorial struggles with the spirit of competition. Leaders who deal with wanting to compete with everyone will always try to intimidate their team members to get ahead. This happens when you're unsure of yourself and jealous of others. When people find it hard to submit, it's a sign that they're territorial. One time I was instructed to train a team of leaders. The person assigned to the lead position gave me a hard time because, in their mind, I was there to take their job. I wasn't there to take their job, but to train them how to become better at their job. After doing my evaluation, I found out that they had a reputation of trying to get rid of anyone who stood in the way of their position. As a result the company never brought in an increase for that department. A person with a territorial mentality hinders his or her own growth and development, which stop them from reaching their full potential. Reaching your potential requires obedience and submission.

When your character is right before God, He will release favor upon your life. Obedience is a reflection of your character. If you are not doing the things in which God has told you it's called immaturity. Immaturity is a state of mind and an act. When you listen, do, and follow then your character is established. People remain immature when they're not teachable.

Immaturity means you're undeveloped mentally, emotionally and spiritually. A person who is immature is a person mentally and emotionally unstable. It means that a person cannot respond to certain situations within an environment person, place, or thing appropriately. Learning how to confront or shall I say respond appropriately is a behavior that generally is caught and taught. If we look at adolescence, we'll find those are the stages when maturity produces, and the teen tries to find balance. Maturity means knowing when to speak up, knowing how to respond, and knowing what to say at the proper time. We must be slow to speak and swift to hear. Maturity also indicates that one has developed a clear comprehension of life intellectually and spiritually. When a leader displays Immaturity is a sign that they're an unteachable person, and it will reflect their character. Sometimes we miss the opportunity to grow because we feel threatened by the person that's been sent to help us. When this happens, you will build a bad reputation.

Leaders who feel threaten

Before going any further, I want to deal with people who are intimidated. Feeling threatened by someone is a character flaw that will destroy your ability to lead. It's a sign that you're insecure and intimidated by their confidence. There were times I've seen people so insecure that people who weren't even confident themselves intimidated them. They saw something in that person or feared the favor upon that person's life. Confidence should always be perfected in stage one. Throughout years of being in ministry, the structure was always set up where leaders were to report back to the headship about the membership. If the team you've chosen haven't dealt with their personal insecurities and feel threaten but someone, they will bring you a negative report. That's why it's good to do meetings with all parties when there is a conflict, just to make sure every word is established properly. Let's examine what happens when you feel threaten a little closely. A person who feels threatened will develop evil intentions and cause pain, injury, damage or create a hostile environment upon someone. It is communicated with intent to bring fear, rejection, isolation or manipulation to gain an advantage over them. Threats are intentional and play on the vulnerability of those you interact with. We must be careful not to develop a vulnerability to the spirit of intimidation. Do a self-evaluation now to see if you're struggling in any of these areas. If you're struggling with two or more, please seek out a mentor, or coach to help you get on track. It doesn't mean you have to step down from Leadership right away. Especially, when you're seeking help.

- Afraid of losing the spotlight
- Afraid of not feeling or being looked at important
- Afraid of submitting to authority
- Afraid of not accomplishing your goal
- Afraid of the consequences of speaking up for what's right

As you can see everyone I've named stems from the spirit of fear. Therefore, if God hasn't given us the spirit of fear (2 Timothy 1:7) we shouldn't allow it to rule over us. When leaders lead through threats, manipulation and fear, it's a sign that their character hasn't been developed and they're headed for a nasty fall.

Developing your character first will prevent you from misleading the people through the spirit of manipulation. Sometimes your vision and desire to fulfill it will become so great that you'll find yourself manipulating the people to do it. Manipulation means to control or influence a person or situation cleverly and unfairly. A manipulator will always twist the situation to suit their needs and find themselves hurting people. Manipulation is often done through the power of perception. A manipulator knows that if they can get you to see what they see; you'll believe in them enough to buy into their lie. You'll find that most people whom battle with this spirit thrives on selfish ambition.

(Philippians 2: -4)

Do nothing out of selfish ambition or vain conceit. Rather, in humility value others above yourselves, not looking to your own interests but each of you to interest others.

Ambitious <u>Webster online defines</u> - to have a strong desire and determination to accomplish something.

We are supposed to be ambitious, especially when pursuing our assignments. But, our ambition can cause us to manipulate others to accomplish our goal. Chasing after people (influence), places (positions), and possessions (power) will always ruin you and keep you in competition with your team. These three areas will always expose what's deeply rooted within us, and what needs to be uprooted out of us.

Identifying the spirit of manipulation working in you.

The heart of a servant

The Bible tells in Matthew 7:15 to beware of false prophets, who come to you in sheep clothing, but inwardly are ravenous wolves. Throughout the years, we've been taught to watch people who always want to get close to the leadership. But wolves are a representation of someone in a leadership position who has disguised themselves as servants. They will give money, and all forms of support but inwardly have a hidden agenda to rob you blind. This form of manipulation will cause you to get out of alignment with your divine assignment; by telling you, you were only created to be obedient to their leadership and vision. They will even go as far as cursing you for deciding to leave or build for your future. I've seen leaders tell their people not to open businesses, not to write books and not to go back to school. They say things like if it's going to inference with you helping me, it's not for you and God won't be pleased with you. This spirit is displayed among those who are clothed with false humility. Manipulating others also carry's a seed of seduction. Seduction means to overly supporting others to get them to lower their defenses to give trust and loyalty to them. (Wikipedia online)

As humans, we are supposed to support others and desire them to trust us and become loyal to us. But the spirit of seduction has an evil intention. Selfish ambition, self-hate, and the spirit of sabotage drive their intention. Those who battle with this spirit must be careful not to fall victim to (Mark 8:36). For what shall it profit a man, if he shall gain the whole world, and forfeit his soul? Sometimes your desire to gain the world becomes so great you misuse God's people to do it.

When the spirit of intimidation is rooted in the leadership, it stops the ministry or organization from advancing to the next level. Promotion is mandatory in our nation. No organization should become comfortable having the same core leadership staff for 20 yrs. Especially if they're looking for massive harvest. The enemy will plant a seed of intimidation within the heart of a leader to stop someone else from moving up the ladder. An example of this happening;

is when a leader who doesn't understand discernment, takes information that hasn't been authenticated to the head; use it, as a character assassination to stop them from being promoted. When Jesus made disciples, He did so with the intent of promoting them to Apostles and for the Apostles to reproduce themselves. Which means, go out and make other leaders. Manipulation will also have you lying on others. A lack of integrity is what I call it.

Lying is defined by <u>Webster online</u>- as communicating non-truth. Lies may be employed to serve a variety of instrumental, interpersonal, or psychological functions for the individual who use them. (<u>Wikipedia</u>)

In 2012 I was blessed with a check for 20,000$. The Lord instructed me to start a small business. But, I was instructed by my leadership not to. After meeting with them, they informed me that I didn't have what it took to start a business and told me the best thing I could do is sow the money into their ministry and wait for God to move. That was the first time I felt the courage and boldness to leave. Sometimes leaders will manipulate the plan that God has given you for their advantage. When this happens, you destroy your own integrity. And integrity is needed to have good character.

Integrity

Integrity <u>Webster online defines</u> - to be righteous, honest, truthful, and having moral principles, good character, and having ethical principles.

One thing I know about integrity is that it is shown in

a person's behavior. Stealing, lying, and cheating are all a lack of integrity. The reason God looks for it is because He holds us all accountable for what we do in and outside of the secret place. Are you doing what is right even when others don't see? It doesn't matter how often you preach, how often you teach if your life isn't preaching integrity it means nothing. A lack of integrity destroys your performance on any job, naturally, and spiritually. It's a character flaw that you aim to destroy. If you were looking to rebound from a lack of integrity the first step would be to create good habits. You can start by sticking to your word. This will bring transformation.

Things you'll need to be transformed.

- Confession
- Surrendering and self-discipline
- Committing to the process of character recovery.
- Learning to confide in someone or accountability.
- Willing to learn something new.

You don't need favor with people who already love you, but for those who don't know you enough to trust you. Favor is released when banks look at your credit and see integrity upon it. When we submit to our process, God will rebuild our character, and through Him, our character will be restored with man. The reason God said obedience is better than sacrifice (1 Samuel 15:22), is because obedience is the momentum that drives us into a position to sanctify. Whenever we sanctify anything, it creates obedience that defines a character of integrity.

We're taught that our life experiences produce

our character. Hardship and how well we deal with confrontation. But just like being a doctor (or any other profession) you must be taught and receive hands-on experiences. It's the same way for developing one's character. The mistake we often make when training leaders is not focusing on their individuality. We do team building exercises to see how well we deal with others and allow that to classify us as leaders or not. The problem with this is that we all can conform, and conforming leads us down a pathway of being fake. Team building exercises are not only designed to see how well you interact with others, but it is an opportunity to see our uniqueness, the thing that makes you different, and help your team win. But we can't teach team building to someone who hasn't embraced his or her true identity. God didn't intend for us to be released into our assignments after being trained. He's wanted to release us after transformation.

Say I relocated or moved to another state to do a job. Upon moving, I needed to find another church home. When I find the church and feels like God wants me planted there, as an Ordained Minister what do I do? Many churches do not honor teaching that you've already had, and many do, (I'm speaking in general). Do I start over as a babe, because I did receive my training there? I believe that when elevated it should be based solely on the transformation of your character and spiritual maturity. Biblical knowledge can be received without a spiritual transformation. Wisdom, revelation, and understanding produce your character and bring forth the transformation that creates sustainable growth. Anytime you are elevated into a new position you will always require training and would I like to call.

Internship. We overlook people because they haven't gone through the ten-year process of training for our leadership? Again, we should look for the transformation of their spirit and character instead. How well they interact and love others, not by the amount of years you've known them, or they've spent in your church or organization.

The disciples were chosen, and they were not trained by any religious system. The Lord trained them. The Word planted in them by Jesus carried more weight than a system created by man. Their training in the Marketplace, (not the church) gave them the experience they needed to be elevated and built their character and reputation among the people. That's why it's important to have a good reputation outside of your organization. In the book of Acts, (Acts 4:13) Peter and John was arrested after healing a man in the name of Jesus. When the leaders, elders, scribes, and high priest came to question them, they called them uneducated and untrained. This was because they had not received formal instruction, training, and teaching from their schools. Therefore, they assumed they didn't know anything. However, they were able to stand up to them with boldness because of the Holy Spirit. They knew who they were, and the power that had been given to them through Jesus name. Now, God is not looking for us to be perfect, but for our motives, intent, and hearts to be pure towards all men. When your heart is pure, and your motives are right, it's a sign of transformation. When your character has been transformed, then you're ready for leadership. The transformation stage will determine the kind of leader you will become. Everyone has a different capacity to lead, and you must be in tune with your capacity. Now let's get back to integrity.

Joseph: was a man full of integrity. He was honest, and had strong moral, principles and was upright. Even though I believe his pride was in him. He still embodied the trait of integrity. Pride was also a key factor that got him rejected and thrown into the pit by his brothers. He was a natural born leader. Now as I stated before all mankind are born to lead. However, some are born with the spirit of leadership upon their lives. Which means some qualities will be a lot stronger in their adolescent years. Leaders who walk with the character trait of integrity walk with cohesion. They are always looking for unity, peace, and love. Joseph had a choice of whether he wanted to uphold his integrity when his master's wife tried to sleep with him. Instead, he fled; keeping his integrity, it cost him. Because of the humiliation, his master's wife felt when Joseph rejected her she lied and got him thrown back into prison. A leader who walks in integrity will always have to pay a price for it.

Martin Luther King Jr was someone I greatly admired. I don't believe I could ever walk in the level of integrity he walked in, especially considering the time he grew up in. I would often say if I were born in that time I would probably be dead. Never in a million years could I walk and allow others to spit on me. Now, I might hear negative comments, name-callings and offenses language coming from the crowds, but I would have needed a strong support system to keep my mouth in check. (Matthew 5:9) Says blessed are the peacemakers for they shall be called the sons of God. His desire to establish peace among all humanity defined his leadership capability and identified him as a son to Christ and defined his character. Not only was he a man of integrity, but full of compassion, love, respect, and honor. He could hold his composure while keeping his integrity and still be confrontational in the midst of adversity. Having possessed all these characteristics made him a triple threat to the enemy. He accomplished the assignment on his life by empowering not only the nation but influencing a government to change. His assignment was to change a system, and when he died, he did just that. He understood the kingdom message and the authority we are to walk in, in spite of the opposition in our time. Living in a culture where people were misusing the doctrine of Christ to enslave an entire race. Martin Luther King Jr was a leader of integrity, compassion excellence, and had a great reputation in his day and ours. He was effective in his gift of ministry and embodied the spirit of leadership in every way he could. One of his greatest lessons we can learn from is his ministry is his ability to stand and fight while maintaining his integrity and keeping his level of composure.

Great tip for building up integrity:

- Always keep your word
- Be a person of standard
- Stand for what's right
- Don't compromise your morals
- Keep your motives pure

Following this list will strengthen your character, and increase your level of influence while your growing into the leader God created you to be.

Compassion

Compassion <u>Webster online defines</u> - as being sympathetic for a person's sufferings misfortunes, being concerned, and warmth. It means to suffer together.

The bible says in (Galatians 6:1) brothers if anyone is caught in any transgressions, you who are spiritual should restore him in a spirit of gentleness. Keep watch over yourself, lest you too be tempted.

Compassion is defined as the feelings that arise when confronted with another's suffering and when you feel motivated to alleviate their pain. Compassion differs from empathy. Empathy is the ability to feel other emotions, whereas compassion is when you feel a desire to help. It is also possible to have compassion for people without helping them. Many researchers have found that being compassionate can improve health, well being, and relationships. Compassion is an action, meaning it activates us to move on people's behalf and removes stress. Compassion also makes us less vindictive towards others. When you learn to show more compassion, you create a positive organization and an environment for your team to feel comfortable. We should aim to be receptive of others and their feelings.

Compassion gives us the ability to understand the emotional, financial, and mental state of another person. Empathy is just the feeling, but we must have a desire to alleviate our brothers and sisters suffering. Empathy places you in a position of understanding what state that people are in. One reason we lack compassion in the world is because we don't know how to see people as individuals and that's the only way to model compassion. A lack of compassion will destroy your reputation. You'll find yourself assuming horrible things about others, being inconsiderate, selfish, and not considering yourself when dealing with others. As leaders, you never want to develop a reputation of not showing compassion on your team.

When you have compassion for others you will never assume the worst about them, be inconsiderate of their feelings and won't be selfish in helping when they're in a time of need. Even though we must have compassion for others, we still must find our inner balance. Not having balance will cause you to become an enabler. Sometime people must experience the fruit of their labor. It's called reaping and sowing. If we create balance in our lives, we would avoid feeling, stressed, overwhelmed and burned out. The Latin meaning of compassion is co-suffering. To have compassion means you notice that people are suffering. Jesus healed, raised people from the dead and fed people through His compassion.

(Matthew 15:32)

Then Jesus called His disciples unto Him and said I have compassion on the crowd because they have been with me now three days and have nothing to eat. And I am unwilling to send them away hungry, lest they faint in the way.

Jesus compassion caused Him to supply the need for the people, which tells us that being moved with compassion opens the doors for miracles. Jesus' motives were always pure concerning His people and His assignment. Our motives help to stabilize our character. Whether you're doing something good or bad, people are always looking for the motives of your heart, to determine if what you're doing is pure. We should embrace the spirit of compassion because we never know if someone lacks support at home, lacks his or her, father/mother, lacks medical treatment, need love, or need healing

When we ignore it, we can't feel compassion, and without compassion, we will never understand, and if we can't understand, we won't help. Everything we go through helps us be relatable to each other. Just because your experience was a walk in the park doesn't mean others are not experiencing difficulties in their life. If we have compassion, we won't judge others so harshly and wrongly. We should never judge or give out advice based on what's best for us. We judge harshly because we lack compassion. Compassion allows us to understand that our imperfections are a part of life. These traits will make us become successful as leaders.

Moses: His character and heart were uncovered when he saw his brother in trouble. When Moses became a grown man, he looked upon his brothers, saw their burdens and was moved with compassion. The next days he saw two men fighting and stepped in and said why are you striking your brother. The leader within him caused him to step up and be a mediator and a peacemaker. These are the leaders we need today. Compassion and being a peacemaker are both character traits that make up a great leader.

Elkanah was a man of compassion. 1Samuel lets us know that Hannah his second wife couldn't have children. Whenever the time would come to make an offering, he would give a portion to both wives. To Hannah, he would give a double portion. Not just because he loved her, but also because she had no children. His compassion for his wife pushed him into a position to be a double blessing to her. Leaders like this will continue to gain followers if they allow the spirit of compassion to lead them.

(Luke 7:13)

And when the Lord saw her, he had compassion on her and said to her, do not weep.

Again Jesus was moved with compassion when he saw a mother weeping as she walks alongside the coffin of her dead son. After being moved by compassion, he told her not to weep, touched the coffin and commanded the man to come forth. When the man came back to life fear fell on the people, and they glorified God. Then the report about Him went out throughout all the surrounding regions. Leaders, who allow their character to encompass compassion, will bring favor and fame to God and themselves.

"A person who encompasses compassion will walk with a sense of excellence in their personal, professional and spiritual life."

Personal and Professional Excellence

Whenever we deal with people, it is very important to create an atmosphere, which allows individuals to feel comfortable in telling personal information about themselves. It is the key to solving their problem. The key is to get people to recognize your value to them. When people are respected and feel confident, they become more reliable and responsible by taking ownership of the vision. They will develop two things, "Personal Excellence, and Professional Excellence."

In every area of life, we try and find balance as the year's approach. Things will always be added and taken away from us. The key to balancing our lives personally and professionally is to be organized and do monthly evaluations on ourselves. This allows us to let go of some things. Sorting out, arranging, and setting order by putting things into categories are some examples of carrying this out. This will allow you to take full control of your life and what is in your space. Here is a list of things that will help build personal and professional excellence and will allow you to flow, focus, and free your mind.

- Analyzing your daily routine
- Assigning your workload into a category
- Arrange into an order
- Separate your emotion to some things
- Eliminate some things

If you work on personal development, you won't become conceited, prideful, or puffed up. It will help you avoid compulsion behavior. Compulsion behavior is a threat to your personal and professional development. It goes back to trying to be a perfectionist. Leaders who battle with compulsion behavior refuse to accept any standard short of what they view as perfection. Compulsion behavior is basically excessive behaviors geared towards persistently and repetitively engaging in activities without leading to an actual reward or pleasure. It means you're never satisfied. This is one of the worst traits to have as a leader. It means you're never satisfied with the work your team can provide. Most leaders who battle with this also have pride. They think no one does it better than them. Daniel had an excellence spirit upon him, which granted him favor with the king. He could only succeed in being excellence because he knew who he was. When your character is developed, and you know who you are, then you can strive to become the best expression of yourself. Becoming the best expression of yourself will enhance your performance on your job, in school, and in ministry.

Personal excellence begins with self-awareness. Self-awareness will help you recognize the areas that you need improvement in. You'll discover your strengths and weaknesses. Self- examination allows you to reflect on your past to track the root cause of your character flaws and failures. When we allow past failures to follow us throughout our lives, it'll block us from embracing personal and professional excellence. Without having the spirit of excellence upon us, we will destroy jobs, and miss out on great opportunities. Developing excellence in these areas will enhance your performance

- ➢ Communication
- ➢ Thinking
- ➢ Dressing
- ➢ Work on your heart
- ➢ Listening skills
- ➢ Recourses
- ➢ Have determination

Geoffrey Canada was a man of personal excellence. He's the CEO/COO of the Harlem Children's Zone in Harlem, New York; an organization whose goal is to increase high school and college graduation rates among those living in Harlem. His determination created his success, wealth and personal excellence. As Dr. Myles Munroe puts it," if you want to be success find a problem to solve". Because of the violence, he endured growing up as a child he was propelled and determined to alleviate the violence in his community. After finishing college, he worked for an organization called Rheedlen Center for Children and Families, which later became Harlem Children Zone. It was such an honor to research him because he is a man who's determined to bring transformation to the world around him. He amplifies empowerment and has created every opportunity not just for the youth but empowers the structure of families across the world. There are so many things we can learn from his personal success and excellence, but I'll name a few. Determination, Persistence, Dedication, Commitment, Reliability, Trustworthy and Servanthood. All of which, made him a great leader whose legacy will be remembered for generations to come. What identified him, as a leader was his act of servanthood and loyalty to his assignment; and desire to go back for his people. When you allow the fruit of God's spirit to take root in your life, it's called "leadership empowerment". The Spirit empowers you to become better in your disposition and personality so others won't assume your feelings or behaviors are bad. When God spirit is not rooted within us, we will misuse our help.

A lack of Professionalism is a sign of an undeveloped leader. It's not something that's fully developed during stage one (character building). People can have qualities of good character, but if they lack leadership development, they'll display unprofessional behavior. Often, people display unprofessional behavior due to bad circumstances. The content of our character is different than the content of our circumstances, which is why we should never be judged based on our circumstances. Even though we shouldn't be judged by them, doesn't give us a pass to treat others harshly. How you interact with others will determine how your team will interact with them. If you are unprofessional with individuals outside your circle, your team will do the same. As a leader, you must model respect and kindness at all times.

Environment is also a key factor when learning how to be professional. Every environment will require something different attitude, appearance, speech, demeanor, and sometimes our hair. Sometimes we're told if we have to change our outward appearance for any platform, it's an indication that the environment is rejecting us. But, I've learned, that is a half-truth. Being professional means, presenting you according to the atmosphere of that environment. In other words, when invited, dress appropriately. Know what to say, when to say it, how to say it, and what the expectations are concerning their dress code. Every establishment has a culture that we must understand. We don't have to take on their beliefs, but we can choose to understand them.

We should make sure we don't send out the wrong signal. When there's disunity within our organization, it lets newcomers know what's accepted. If your core leadership doesn't look presentable, it sends a signal to the newcomers that anything will eventually be accepted. Study these key points if you're looking to grow in excellence and professionalism.

- Don't just be on time, but participate.
- Demonstrate excellence among your team.
- Be respectful of others time. Value your teammates.
- Always follow protocol and instruction.
- Learn the dress code of that environment and adapt.
- Protect your ears from negative thoughts, and embrace a positive attitude.

Remember if you want favor, you must show kindness and be courteous. God will never force anyone to bless you. In order for us to have favor, there must be an opportunity given to us by others, (God uses people to bless people). Only your character will stop others from blessing you, not your circumstances.

Leadership

Because of the old nature, as humans, we must always be renewed. Many of us don't believe in continued repentance or daily deliverance. The new emerging leaders that God intends to use are those who focus on crucifying the old man. I was taught to blame the enemy for everything that happened to, especially when my money or body was hit. We say things like, "lying devils". But, after much biblical research, I found out that the enemy has no power to stop us. 1John 3:8 says whoever makes a practice of sinning is of the devil, for the devil has been sinning from the beginning. The reason the Son of God appeared was to destroy the works of the devil.

The works of the enemy have been rendered powerless. When you grow in God and acknowledge who you are, nothing can stop you. Although, the enemy doesn't have power to destroy you he will conspire against the old man that's deeply rooted within you, to get you to crucify the new man that's emerging. The manifestation of the earth and all its habitats are a result of the mind of God. In order for us to carry out God's vision upon the earth, we need the mind of Christ to do it. Operating in the mind of Christ requires a change of heart.

(**Psalm 51:10**) says Create in me a clean heart, O God, and renew a right spirit within me.

In this hour God is shifting and releasing an outpouring of His spirit among new vessels. There is a different harvest, and it's going to take a different leadership to usher them in. We can't get stuck in the old move we must embrace the new. The world is tired of the traditions in our churches. To be honest, many believe religion is bringing a separation within the world. One thing I've learned is that we can't continue to fight the old traditions with wrong ammunition. Why? Because new traditions forming every year trying to stop the glory of God from being revealed. We need the truth and revelation of the hour to push us all the way through. Old traditions continue to linger on the surface, but there are new ones growing. A house divided against itself cannot stand. This is why the enemy fights against us. He wants to divide us. When Christ comes back for His body, He's not looking for one or two churches, but He's looking for those who are birth in His culture. Religion will have local churches preparing people to live in an isolated kingdom; separated from the world, when our job is to influence them. God wants us to be one and think like one. Old wineskin is a representation of an old move, which are controlled by old vessels. A generation who've become stuck in their way of thinking, dull of hearing and those whose hearts have become hardened because of pride.

When Old wineskin gets old, it would dry up and get hard. It loses it elasticity and won't expand causing a crack when the new wine is poured into it. This, however, doesn't mean it can't be repaired. Which means, the old man doesn't need to be thrown away but reconditioned (repaired). Recommitting to a process of transformation is what God requires. Taking old wineskin through a reconditioning stage will help it expand and become flexible again. The process includes submerging it under water then rubbing oil on it. The same process is required for those in leadership.

Leaders who submerge themselves with the washing of the Word and consecrate themselves will always stay current with the moves of His Spirit. The vessels must be open and able to retain new revelation. Consecrating yourself will break the hardness of your heart and without it; there could be a spiritual resistance, keeping you locked in traditions. New wine skinners will expand their capacity to receive more. There is a constant desire for an outpouring of His Spirit upon them. Only the Holy Spirit can create in you a clean heart and renew in you a right spirit. Each process you go through is designed to restore the old wineskin, (the old vessel/ person). The old and new are not going to always agree, which is why the old leadership will fight against new emerging leaders. Without our leaders having discernment their hearts and minds will remain stuck in a dullness state. Having dullness will cause you to develop a blockage and stop you from receiving. That's why there must be a constant renewing. The word renews means to make new again. It means to complete a process in one stage and go higher in another stage.

John 2:12 on the third day there was a wedding at Cana of Galilee, and the mother of Jesus was there. Jesus also was invited to the wedding with his disciples. When the wine ran out, the mother of Jesus said to him, they have no wine. And Jesus said to her, Woman, what does this have to do with me? My hour has not yet come. His mother said to the servants, do whatever he tells you. Now there were six stone water jars there for the Jewish rites of purification, each holding twenty or thirty gallons. Jesus said to the servants, fill the jars with water. And they filled them up to the brim. And he said to them, now draw some out and take it to the master of the feast. So they took it. When the master of the feast tasted, the water now become wine, and did not know where it came from (though the servants who had drawn the water knew), the master of the feast called the bridegroom, and said to him, everyone serves the good wine first, and when people have drunk freely, then the poor wine. But you have kept the good wine until now. This, the first of his signs, Jesus did at Cana in Galilee, and His disciples believed in Him.

We must first look at what a wedding represents. A wedding represents unification, a joining, and a merging. When you think of a person getting married, you think about newness, a name change, and a dying to oneself. It's a time where both parties agree to join for a greater purpose. They become one, yet still, understand that someone is to take the lead. It's a time of celebration and a time of crossing over. Now, the releasing of the new wine is a joining of the Holy Spirit and the church. The Holy Spirit is the person that helps us to become one with God. He renews, refreshes and reprograms us so we can have the mind of Christ. The Greek meaning of church is **Ekklesia**, which means a people called out or set apart. It means we belong to the Lord. There are many angles we can look at this; nevertheless, we will focus on His Spirit. Now we see Mary approaching Jesus about their lack of wine at the wedding. Jesus then informs her that His hour had not yet come. By revelation, Jesus wasn't referring to the miracle of supplying natural wine, but to the outpouring of His Spirit. His Spirit is symbolic of the new wine that was set to be released upon His death burial and resurrection. That's why on the day of Pentecost when the Holy Spirit was released there were people standing by mocking the church saying they were full of new wine. In Jesus act of obedience to His mother, He instructed them to fill the six water pots (that were sitting reserved for the purification of the Jews) with water to the brim. The six containers were set aside for their traditions. The number six is significant for the number of man's work. It symbolizes man's weakness and their abilities. Instructing them to fill the water pots to the brim with water was symbolic of a spiritual cleansing that can only happen from within and by the washing of the Holy Spirit, not their traditions. In Mark 7:1 the Pharisees and scribes came together to question Jesus about His disciple eating bread with unwashed hands. Jesus rebukes them, letting them know there is nothing that enters a man from outside, which can defile him; but only the things which come out of him. The old wineskin loses it elasticity and breaks down because of its inward traditions. We must be cleansed from the inside. The new wine cannot be received upon people who've become complacent in their traditions. When the master of the feast tasted the wine, he could recognize the new, meaning something he wasn't familiar with, never tasted or accustomed to. The wine given to the master was Jesus way of saying the leadership must shift first. To recondition the old vessels (leadership), they must go through a spiritual soaking and be submerged in oil. Submit to a time of consecrating themselves in Christ, rebuilding their character and embracing their leadership capabilities. This allows them to be reminded of their assignment to the world. Many have been leading from a position of their tradition, not His Spirit. When you're leading from a traditional perspective, it means you're out of alignment with Gods timing and will miss the revelation of the hour.

What is a leader?

People say that being a leader is based on having influence over a group of people. But, the first sign of a leader is understanding what you were created to sacrifice for our world. Becoming an effective leader requires personal development. It's a process of finding your identity. Effective leaders are leaders transformed by the renewing of their minds. Their minds must be delivered from things that tried to rob them of their identity before they can lead others effectively. After learning your identity, the next thing a leader must do is build relationships. One night as I was preparing for bed when I realized. "You can't be an effective leader until you learn how to effectively build relationships".

When Jesus came, the first thing he did was established relationships. Building relationships is what teaches you how to love and respect people. Learning them helps us understand them a lot more. Whenever a person can't effectively build relationships, it's a reflection of their ability to lead. Many leaders will lead based on power and position when they are broken. They will demand respect instead of earning it because earning it requires building relationships. Often, we go through life with secrets and hidden agendas when we're broken. We must lead based on our character, and building relationships with others help validate us as a leader.

Leaders are people and take's time to learn more about them and their difference. What they're sensitive to and what will likely offend them. Exceptional leaders will set out to understand cultural environment and the effects it has on us as a people. They seek an integrated mindset. His or her goal is to build everyone whose heart is open, ready, and willing. Everyone is important, and shouldn't be left out. If you don't utilize every member of your team, you won't be able to add value to your people. This sanction will give you key information about leadership and how to help your team grow to the next level.

Leaders

Learning	Earn	Achieve	Develop	Empower
↑	↑	↑	↑	↑
Keep	Respect	Success	Leaders	Everyone

Leading your teams based on your relationship will cancel out discord confusion and offense. Most of the problems I've encountered in ministry were not from the head but from those acting on behalf of the head. I was held back many times because the leader was given false information about me from their leadership staff. As

I cried out to the Lord for understanding He helps me to see things from a different perspective. I had to realize the role of leadership. In between the Headship and the people is the leadership. Leadership is the bridge that seals the gap in communications. When I worked for this restaurant, I remember my manager calling me into a meeting. He wanted to know if there were any complaints coming f,rom the customers and he was looking for suggestions on how to better serve them. He asked me because I was the bridge between him and the people.

There were times people would complain about our prices, but I was there to help them understand why we charged what we charged. I didn't get mad and say if you're not for us leave. We needed their service, and they needed ours. Leaders who walk in true teamwork will bring peace and understanding between the head and the people. The people on the lower level may not have a full understanding of things and complain to delegated authority. However, delegated authority must be the bridge that brings peace and helps others crossover and connect to the vision. If the leaders you've chosen are not equipped to understand the cry or the need of the people, they will bring you a negative report concerning them. Accurate communication is very critical for leaders. We must engage in every conversation with discernment, positive perception, compassion and an open mind and heart. The bridge (leadership) between the headship and the people has been broken for many years. What we need now, more than ever in our churches and nations are leaders who are spirit lead and in tune with the heart of God. Learning how to process communication should be a part of every leadership developmental process. If you're going to train up great leaders, you should focus on their character along with their listening skills, how well they follow instructions, communication, and organizational skills.

Developing these set of skills will help you become a better follower. Leaders will never be great, without learning to follow. Learning how to follow is what get you promoted to the next level. During this process, you will usually gain more insight to help your team and insight into their character. Learning their character will teach you how to communicate with them, and trust them. The disciples learned organizational skills when Jesus instructed them to make the people sit in groups before feeding the four and five thousand. Embracing these set of skills will open the door for more to come into your life.

Visionary leaders

Every leader who plans to lead cannot lead until his/her vision has properly aligned. God asked Jeremiah what do you see. He was training him to be a visionary leader. Although you may be a visionary leader it's important to remember that your vision can only be accomplished through those who you trust to run with it. Throughout the years, I've seen many leaders keep the vision a secret from the team. Some people find it hard to give their time and resources to things they don't understand. The vision comes before the push. Without people understanding the vision they cannot help you push it out. Your leaders must be connected to the vision first. They must be married to it. "Sight of the vision doesn't come when it's visible on paper, but when it's received in your heart".

Writing the vision and making it plain is very important for seeing your vision come to pass. Always put all the details down of what you see and hear in your mind. If you write it down, you can go over it to make sure it's what you desire to see happen. Next, recite the vision so those who are connected can be able to say it word for word with clarity and understanding. Don't allow your team to run for you without them being able to fully understand it. You must translate your vision with clarity. Next, give them time to shift, recite it repeatedly, and do a quarterly evaluation to make sure your team still understands it. When you do, they will run more effectively and more forcefully, without being tainted. If your vision is tainted, they'll be running in the wrong direction, and everything that you're building will collapse. Over the years many leaders have failed because they've sent their teams out with a tainted vision. Not, because it wasn't clear enough, but because it was tainted by their wrong thinking and environment. Therefore, make sure your thinking is influenced by the right people, places, and things. When you do, it will help your team be more productive.

Leaders must become acquainted with two things, their strengths, and their weaknesses. These are the two areas that will hinder you. As leaders, we're required to grow people, and teach them how to build with their strengths, and overcome their weaknesses. Basically, find balance in their emotions. When your emotions are out of whack, it will throw your vision off. "Leaders are visionaries that trust their team to run with the vision."

Keys to becoming a great leader

Great Leaders focal points:

- Prepared- ready at all time
- Proactive- look for a way to stay ahead
- Alert and aware of what's going on around you
- Learn how to release trust to others

Responsibility of great leaders

- Restore the vision of the lost
- Help them to understand commitment
- Help restore relationships among the people
- Teach discipline
- Teach them self-value
- Self-control
- Restoring passion

Four characteristics that great leaders possess

- Process- not impatient
- Power- no how to give it away without being intimidated
- Purpose- doesn't start till they understand what the result will be
- Persuasion- understand the power of persuading the people to buy into the vision

One reason people don't like to go through the process is because they don't understand these four areas. This generation of leaders wants to know what's going to be given to them, and the purpose it will serve.

Key point for great leaders

- Leaders are followers.
- Leaders follow instructions.
- Leaders speak up and ask questions.
- Leaders are deliverers
- Leaders embrace the vision.
- Leaders know learn their measure.
- Leaders build relationships
- Leaders who're not intimidated by their team.
- Leaders value other's ideas.

These are just a few traits that'll help you along the way. Leader's who focus on their assignments will develop good character traits to strengthen themselves. You are responsible for your own growth and development. You must be committed to learning more. There is a phase I use to hear growing up, that says, leaders are readers. You can't grow without learning, and learning requires reading. Use the list of words above to study your character as a leader. Define each word on a sheet of paper, then make a commitment to yourself to change what needs to be changed. Now let's examine the different types of leaders.

Training Leaders

Now there was a woman named Hannah. She prayed earnestly to the Lord about a child. After a while, the Lord came upon her womb, and she conceived and bore a son whom she promised to give back to the Lord. After the birth of her son, as she promised she took him to the priest Eli to minister before the Lord. Samuel's first prophecy was to his leader, and it wasn't a pretty word. Because Eli took the time to teach, train, and develop Samuel when the Lord spoke to him about his leader he wasn't intimidated by him.

When you take the time to build a relationship with people it makes it easier to perceive what spirit they are coming from. Even though Eli had issues, he could perceive what spirit was leading Samuel because he took time to establish a firm, solid relationship with him. As leaders, we should teach them how to analyze every download given to them.

Discipline leaders

Leaders are discipline and are not controlled by their emotions. They don't put themselves in compromising positions. They're not rebellious. They listen to those they're submitted to. When leaders are disciplined, they walk with integrity. They're purpose driven and will become more passionate about their assignment. They don't waste time going over things that mature people should have perfected while strengthening their character.

Leaders who investigate

Whenever a crime is committed in the world, the police have special teams who investigate. Even they know that only gifted, trained, and people who're passionate about their gift can find hidden clues. Drug dealers have a lookout person to watch their backs. What am I saying? Leaders need investigators on their teams, a lookout person. People see what they're not able to see. Those we like to call the watchers on the wall. The lookout person is responsible for notifying the leader of the gang when the police are coming on the scene. As watchers, we can detect pitfalls and threat trying to sneak into our camp. Therefore, leaders must recognize what each member on their team is capable of and use them accordingly. A leader is not a leader until he utilizes and unleashes the potential within his team. It's not a one-sided relationship. He or she needs you to fulfill their assignment as a leader, and you need them to reach your assignment as a potential leader. They teach you how to captivate your gifts, and create a lifeline of support for growth and development. The more you develop yourself, as a leader the more insight will be given. You can't grow without being stretched out of the confines of your comfort zone. So it's important to find your circle, and invest in them.

Protector Leaders

As leaders, we must protect our people against foolishness and false accusations. When people can recognize the protector in you, it will open the door for more influence and allows you to empower more people to change. About fifteen years ago I was working at a restaurant that had no system in place to protect their employees. The saying back then was, all customers were right. There was no room for error, but a huge opening for false accusations. One time a customer came in and lied on one of my coworkers because their fries were not hot enough, well, we were told to call the manager. When the manager came, she called my coworker and went off in front of the customer than fired her. After that, the manager lost all respect for the other employees. People started calling off, walking off and not working to their full capacity. When your team doesn't feel protected they won't respect you as their leader or be effective on your team anymore. So embrace the protector in you.

Carnal Leaders

Paul dealt with the carnalities about the perspective of the leaders whom he addressed in the letter to the church. He speaks of three areas that will indicate a carnal leader. One who starts up *envy, strife*, and *division?* As a leader, when someone on your team comes to you with an issue and your first response is to go to the head with an opinion of your own, (without all the facts & truth) implementing your assumptions. You're not ready for leadership. Let's go over these three.

Envy: a feeling of discontentment and covetousness regarding another advantages, success, and possession. Envy is one most potent cause of unhappiness. Because they're unhappy, they'll try and inflict that same pain on someone else. Psychologists have recently suggested there may be two types of envy: malicious envy and benign envy—malicious envy proposed as a sick force that ruins a person and his/her mind and causes the envious person to blindly want the "hero" to suffer; benign envy proposed as a type of positive motivational force that causes the person to aspire to be as good as the "hero"-but only if benign envy is used in a right way.

There are so many leaders wounded because of the spirit of envy. This is a seed that's sown into its victim from past hurts, lack of confidence, lack of attention, lack of self-accomplishment and just never feeling satisfied. I've been a part of organizations where the leadership developed a negative assumption about the newcomers. A lot of times they reminded them of someone who had hurt them in the past. However, just because that person reminds you of past hurts doesn't give you the right to mistreat them, when they have chosen to follow you. A leader should never allow themselves to be so wounded that they become envious and try to destroy everything that another person is building. One time I was leading a team when one member didn't like me being chosen to lead. So, every time we would come together they wouldn't cooperate. When a leader operates in this spirit, they are not equipped to lead. Their mindset is, if I can't do what I want to do or be the leader, I rather let it fall. Leaders should never strive to out beat other team members. When you're working on a team, there's no room for competition or being envious of each other's gifts.

Strife: angry, bitter disagreement over fundamental issues; conflict. Strife brings in discord confusion and seeks to destroy its prey. That's right, I said its PREY! A person who stirs up strife does it with evil intentions. It stems from jealousy and insecurities. Those who operate in this spirit is also very competitive. If there's one thing I know, is that there's no room for hate in our world. We are living in a time where murder and death have become the highlight of our days. Evil has corrupted the hearts of many men and women; even our children have developed a spirit of hate towards one another. When a leader doesn't submit to strengthening their character and don't deal with the issues of their past, they become bitter. Bitterness will cause you to display disrespectful behavior towards others, that leads you to stir up strife. Leaders who embody this trait will infect other leaders and those who're not in leadership positions.

There are six things that the Lord hates, seven that are an abomination to him: haughty eyes, lying tongue, and hands that shed innocent blood, heart that devises wicked plans, feet that make haste to run to evil, false witness who breathes out lies, and one who sows discord among brothers. (Pro: 16-19)

The definition for discord is strife, and the Lord considers it to be an abomination. So now let's observe it from a leadership position.

- Leaders with haughty eyes – arrogant and full of pride
- Leaders with a lying tongue – lacks integrity, doesn't speak up, spread false accusations
- Leaders quick to shed innocent blood – no mercy, quick to throw others under the bus

- Leaders with a heart that devises wicked plans – evil intention/motives
- Leaders who feet are quick to run to evil – don't waste any time crucifying others
- Leaders false witnesses -willing to lie for others
- Leaders who sow discord among the brothers – one who stirs up confusion

Division – the action of separating something into parts, or being separated. Its disagreements between two or more groups, typically producing tension or hostility. Wherever you find division, you will always find a spirit that tries to inflict a state of isolation among the people. For you to complete the assigned project that you're working on with your team, it will require you to work in unity. The nation is in a state of division right now. Racism is at an all-time high. A least for our time; and to be honest, I don't know if I believe that it will get better. Each day we're faced with the fears of terrorist attacks. Again, a house divided against itself cannot stand. Due to the hatred in our country, I'm afraid that it leaves us open for a major attack. If we don't embrace the spirit of unity the world, we know it will soon fade away. Yes, I'm speaking to an end. We are living in different times, and no group of people will allow themselves to be enslaved by any force. Slavery, however, has found. It's comfort in another form, just to divide us. The prisons, the schools, the workplace, and even our ministries have been infiltrated with this spirit called division. For this spirit to be uprooted we must learn to work together. Notice I didn't say sit back and pray, I said work. Faith without works in dead. That mean, we can't just sit back and pray, we must act on what we receive from God.

There must be a plan in place to benefit us all as a whole. I don't believe in compromising, by taking away the rights of a people to satisfy another group of people. I believe we all have choices. God never takes away our rights, He wants us to choose Him. He forces no one to submit to His laws, and neither should we. We must teach those who want to know our culture and keep it moving. Jesus didn't force the kingdom on anyone. He never went into government and commended the laws to be changed, he just inspired and empowered them to develop the culture of the kingdom. Teaching them the kingdom culture and sending them out to empower others is what silence the existence of other cultures. Leaders whose character is weak run the risk of setting an example of division and discord because of their lack of integrity. We need leaders who are peacemakers to lead our churches, communities, and our nations.

Leaders with hidden agendas

There a Man of God was instructed by the Lord to go to Bethel to deliver a word. God commanded him not to stop and fellowship with anybody. But while he was there the son of an old prophet went home and told the prophet (their father) all the works that the man of God had done. And the words he had spoken to the king. The prophet was impressed and set out to find the man of God. Now two things impressed the old prophet. His works and favor to with the king. So, the lying prophet saddled his donkey and went out to greet him. As he approached Him, he told the Man of God to come to his house. But the Man of God replied, no and told him what instruction God had given him. (1 Kings 13:11) The lying Prophet informed him that it was ok. So the young prophet decided to go.

Here we see the characteristics of someone with a hidden agenda, wrong motives. The man was only impressed at his ability to hear from God and his favor with the king. When the Man of God went with him (based on lies from the lying prophet), he lost his life. We must be very careful of leaders with hidden agendas. They're only plans of connecting is to rob you of the favor and influence upon your life. These leaders don't study or invest in themselves enough to grow ahead. They have an unteachable spirit and flow in manipulation. Beware, lest they come to get you out of alignment with your assignment.

Hidden agendas

- People with hidden agendas would always let something fall instead of allowing someone else to receive credit for it. If they can't have it, nobody else will.
- People with hidden agendas deal with the spirit of control. Everything must be their way.
- People with hidden agendas deal with the spirit of seduction, deliberately enticing a person, to lead them astray. They're always looking to lead you to destroy you.

- People with hidden agendas have a lazy spirit. They're always looking for someone else to do the work.
- People with hidden agendas are attracted to the image. They'll always go after people that appear to have a lot going for themselves. They will use their connections (people of high-esteem, big name) to impress you.

These leaders have a lot of contacts, but few connections, and no real influence. Meaning, they may know people, but because of their inability to build solid relationships, they can't move to the next level. The right connections will come and take them higher when they learn how to be relational. Their resume alone cannot get them to where they're going. If you stay, honest influence will just increase. Leaders should never give an alternative to the truth!

Authentic Leadership

Authentic leaders are self-actualized individuals aware of their strengths, their limitations, and their emotions. They don't act one way in private and another way in public. They don't hide their weakness they perfect them. They are mission-driven and focused on results. They put the mission and goals of the company ahead of their own. They know who they are, and refuse to conform to who others want them to be. They're not in it for money, power, or ego but results.

- They lead with their heart.

- They focus on the long-term results.
- They flow in transparency.
- They are processors (their thoughts).

An Authentic person isn't false or copied. They're genuine, real, trustworthy, rely on facts, truthfulness, not they're not a counterfeit.

Today we are missing authentic leaders. Most leaders are being trained to flow in someone else's anointing. It's important that we remember that each person is unique and has a uniqueness to their gifts and callings. The anointing contributes to the growth and development of the gifts. Whenever leaders focus is to get people to imitate them, they lose sight of the kingdom assignment. God told Jeremiah He knew him when he was in the womb. He called him before earth experienced him. God was trying to get Jeremiah to understand that he was called to be authentic. Before you start an assignment to lead you must accept yourself first.

Transformational Leadership

Transformational leaders challenge their teams how to take ownership of their work. Giving them tasks that will enhance their performance and inspire each member to grow. As leaders, we should:

- Encourage our people to be innovative and creative (new ideas).
- Look for individual contributions (their ideas and input).
- Challenge them to leave their comfort zones.

- Teach them how to believe in their abilities.
- Be a role model.

Transformation means to change the foundation of your thinking. It's a conversion that will transform your mind back into an authentic being. True transformation builds character and lays a solid foundation to birth the things of God. (Romans 12:2) Be transformed by the renewing of your mind. The reason the children of Israel couldn't see themselves in the promised land is because their minds hadn't been renewed. However, God called them forth because he knew what he had placed inside them. As humans, we were created for the sole purpose of leading, and just because we have flaws in our character doesn't mean we won't accomplish them. Our character positions us to access the favor for our future. Another reason transformation is important is because some people develop a poverty mindset overtime that affects their character. Wealth doesn't classify a person as being free from a poverty mentality. Often, we make negative decisions due to our minds being locked in a state of poverty. There are marriages failing daily because the mate was chosen based on a poverty mindset. Example: being raised in poverty one might tell themselves that the only way to feel the void of their insecurities is to find people who look like they desire to be. This is dangerous because you can run into someone with a false spirit and just as shallow as like you.

Captivating teams

Captivating the ideas of your team means taking an interest in their ideas. Not hindering them by keeping them under the confines of your vision. You are a part of a team; a team comes together as one to achieve a common goal or purpose. It means they collaborate and submit to one another. They have a mutual understanding to serve so both can bring an increase. Here is a list of things transformational leaders will do to captivate their teams.

- Set goals
- Solve problems
- Make decisions
- Responsible
- Accountable
- Responsive
- Difference of opinion and perspective is valued.

Leaders are born

Many researchers say leaders are made. However, certain traits allow us to identify future leaders. Anyone can emerge as a leader among a group, but not everyone can perform at a top level. Which means leaders must be made. Simply put everyone needs training. Some may have a capacity to handle small groups where others will have a larger capacity to lead nations.

Although we all are destined for leadership, to perform effectively in a position you must be made. Whenever we chose leaders who haven't gone through a process, we should never get mad when they don't perform or live up to our expectations. Sometimes we choose leaders based on their charisma and perceived intelligence. That's a joke! Whatever happened to a person's character? You were predestined with purpose before you were born to lead. That's why the Bible says many are called, but few are chosen. Although you are called, you will not be chosen until you learn to submit to a teacher. You must be able to effectively operate in that role to accomplish everything God intended you to accomplish. Our life experiences and proper teaching is what produces our character. A character that gives us the qualifications we must operate in to be a leader. Not allowing the process to develop and qualify you to fulfill that role can cause delays, hindrances, and setbacks.

- Leaders are born with certain charismatic gifts.
- A lack of training will cause some to conform –vs.- lead?
- Assuming responsibility comes from the heart, and some people are born with an instinct to assume responsibility.
- Assuming responsibility it what makes you a great leader.

Samuel: Leaders who know God's voice and understand who they are and not be intimidated by those they're assigned to groom.

Esther: Leaders must have courage, and understand why they were given power and influence. Esther had to realize that it wasn't about her, but something much greater. When you put others needs before your own God can use you for greater. If you are a leader, who functions in any governmental office having wisdom when dealing with people is a key essential when leading. You should always have the intent to help them. We need leaders who can shift us into alignment and lead us. Those who are mature and full of revelation and revelation simply speak of a new vision. Having the vision to see ahead. Before you can operate in any leadership capacity, you must understand the importance of living a life governed by wisdom and vision. Without the spirit of wisdom, you won't be able to help others identify their purpose or potential. Therefore, you won't be effective when leading them. Esther loved people and her intentions were pure, which made her a great leader.

Here is a list: of words to that will help bring awareness to you so you won't be so judgmental of others and fall victim to self-dysfunction. God's wisdom will help you to understand and have compassion on the world.

Dysfunction- Dysfunction comes into a person's life because of a lack of self-control. A lack of self-control is a sign of immaturity and stops you from growing. Immaturity can cause major dysfunctions in a person's life. Dysfunctional behavior is a personality disorder that speaks to your pattern of thoughts. It stops you from being relational with other, which can stop your growth & development. A person who operates in this spirit will never connect to the vision because they have trouble perceiving and coming into agreement with you. When dysfunction is seen within a person, it means the seed has already taken root within them. This seed is sown to bring about confusion discord and disunity within your teams. If the seed of dysfunction lives in your heart and mind, you'll lose respect with them. This is a dangerous seed to look out for when you're trying to grow in leadership.

Dishonest- this seed is design to destroy you and your view of people. It may seem like it's just centered on people who lie, but this seed has a greater intention. Being dishonest can shut down discipleship, growth/ development. When you have a negative perception about those you have been sent to help, sometimes you won't help. When a leader falls victim to this seed, his discernment about that person becomes blurry, and that person is left in their infancy stages of growth. God never reveals a negative flaw to a person that's not mature enough to bear it. Leadership cannot train people who don't trust them.

Distractions- a distraction comes to cloud your judgment. Leaders need wisdom when building people and infrastructures. When a leader gets distracted, he causes his own destruction. Let's think of it this way. If you're building blocks and get distracted every block you've built will fall and potentially break. Distractions are a sign that your discernment has been tainted. Therefore, you should never trust the information you've been given until you have carefully processed it. You may also need someone whose skilled to help you go through the process. Leaders that are easily distracted will lead you in the wrong direction. Make sure you're not leading from a place distraction.

Disruptive behavior- Disruptive behavior is a seed sown to bring disunity. It's implemented to create an uncooperative mindset to stop the progression of our ministries, organizations, and communities. Disruptive behavior is a sign of an unteachable person. If we're not teachable to the leaders in our lives, it may be a sign that we're not teachable with God. No one wants to work with people who don't listen or try to follow instructions. Unteachable leaders are prideful and will lose their respect.

Depression- Depression is a brain disorder characterized by persistent loss of interest in activities causing significant impairment in daily life. Confusion comes and keeps you locked in a state of depression to bring dysfunction in the mind. To be productive and persistent in our daily lives we must be free from depression. Sometimes having someone to hold you accountable will help you keep a clear perception. When a person reaches a state of depression, it means something tragic watered it, and now it has taken root within them. When this happens, only deliverance will set you free. Wisdom cannot find rest in a person with a root of depression growing inside. Leaders who suffer from depression will be in danger of leaving their teams behind in a crisis.

Demoralizing- Demoralizing means to deprive a person of spirit, courage, and to bring disorder and confusion upon someone. It also means to corrupt or undermine the morals of a person. Listen! demoralizing someone comes from a person who flows in jealousy, intimidation, fear, and rejection. The person will often use their influence to gain the attention of those in authority to defame a person's character. They are driven by their emotions. You cannot discern a character flaw on someone when you have already displayed a negative perception about that person. When someone intimidates you, it can cause you to become paranoid. When this happens, your discernment becomes paralyzed. If a leader finds themselves demoralizing their teams, they'll never win the battle.

Great Leaders who shaped our nation.
Madam C J Walker

Madam C J Walker invented hair care products. She was an entrepreneur and a true visionary at heart. She was a visionary whose sole reason for inventing hair care products was to solve a problem for her and others. She found her purpose, one that created wealth for her life and a legacy that's benefitting our generation and generation to come. She was a risk-taker graced with favor to break the traditions of her time. Because of her dedication, she crafted a product that changed the face of women, and establish confidence and perfected a greater inner beauty in the women of our culture. She was well respected, strong, educated, and a leader of excellence.

Harriet Tubman

Harriet Tubman was a civil war nurse and civil rights activist who acted as a spy for the United States Army and a world-renowned humanitarian. She is described as a woman of courage, a warrior, influencer, and risk-taker. She was responsible for rescuing seventy families enslaved by a corrupt system of leaders. Leaders who were tainted due to racism and hatred. She led thirteen mission trips using safe houses that created systems called *The Underground Railroad* to free slaves. Here's what we can learn from her story as leaders.

- Not to be afraid when the system is against you
- Stand when no one else will

- Your assignment will be connected to solving other people's problems
- Your resources may be in others
- Be connected to the people that are going to fight with you and for you

Albert Einstein

Albert Einstein was one of the most celebrated scientists of the Twentieth Century. His profound theories it what laid the framework for physics. He was a humanitarian who not only spoke out against nuclear weapons but also was involved in the campaign to end lynching. He also supported the state of Israel. Although he followed no established religion he found a strong connection between religion and science, His opinion of God created a harmony between the two. He is known as the greatest genius of the Twentieth Century. Early academic years reveal his lack of interest in learning. He stated that he wanted to learn what he wanted to know, and the normal routine of school boards him. There's so much to learn about his leadership, but I'll only list a few.

- Leaders who know who they are and don't conform to social standards
- Leaders who see no limits
- Leaders with revolutionary thinking
- Leaders who get involved in the world around them
- Leaders who find their sense of purpose

Character and leadership building teaches you values, morals, help you establish ethics, principles that determine how your gifts will be affected. The first step to embracing your gift is to desire the spirit of leadership and developing habits that increase your ability to perform at a level of personal excellence. Walking in humility, joy, love, peace, and inner respect will create the confidence to gain influence across the world. Because of my love for God, and His creation I pushed myself these last few years to create a habit of self- discipline. Regardless of the challenges I've faced, or still facing nothing can stop me from being the best me I can be. Just like the bible says you must desire to prophesy, you must desire to grow in leadership and desire a better character. My desire every day is to have the spirit of leadership. God will never place a demand on something He never put inside of you. A greater demand is placed on the gifts and callings when we are mature enough to carry the assignment. Our calling is connected to His purpose. So, learning what His purpose is for our lives is key to being developed. We are born with the characteristic of our calling. When God calls us He speaks into our spirit, and our spirit ignites a physical response. Many times I tried to reject my call to lead because of what people thought about me. I was told until you have produced yourself in three people you're not equipped to lead. But Jesus was promoted into a leadership position before He reproduced Himself in anyone, which means we cannot limit ourselves. To grow as leaders, you also must be given a chance to lead. Let's end this section with a few points about character and leadership qualities.

- Sometimes knowing the reputation, you have among others gives you the power to change
- Humility is a character trait that you can developed
- The seed of partiality will destroy your team
- Christ served those who weren't on His level
- Character is the first thing we develop, and the first thing others encounter
- Strengthening your character is a choice
- The first sign that you're ready to lead is being free from your past
- Control takes away your trust
- Influence empowers your choice
- Jesus recruited leaders and trained them to be servants
- Do regular self- check-ups

Team leaders

A team is a group of individuals who come together to accomplish a goal. They are not in competition with each other, and their focus is complimenting one another. Once you've trained your leaders, it's now time to establish your teams to carry out the assignment. Sharing the work means sharing the responsibility and authority. Jesus sent His disciples out two by two, so building strong team won't hinder you, but will advance you. Anytime you establish a team it's always wise to place people whose skills complement one another on the team. It's important that each member can perform according to his or her skills. Each member should also be given a measure. Following instructions will always increase their capacity to do more, so leave the door to do more open. That's why we must evaluate them before placing them on a team. Again, everyone accomplishes tasks differently, and when a person is forced to stay within the confines of a position they've outgrown, they become frustrated. When leaders give their people tasks that enhance their performance, you both receive an increase. Leaders who train their teams to operate in these six areas will increase their productivity and stability.

Leader

- **L**- Longevity- life expectancy
- **E**- Endurance- staying in the fight or a difficult journey even when they haven't seen to victory yet.
- **A**- Advantage- knowing what your strengths and weaknesses are, what on your teams and using them to win.
- **D**- Dependability- having integrity and counting on each other. If your plan fails, not being afraid to brainstorm with the rest of the team to do it.
- **E**- Engage- learning how to draw from one another and making sure you do your part. Teamwork is not about making sure your work is complete, but making sure the whole assignment is complete.
- **R**- Risk-taker- not being afraid to take challenges in the midst of losing it all. Simply put believing in each other and what each other bring to accomplish your victory.

Sometimes things don't work out, not because they're out of order, but because they can't carry the measure they have been given. Measure is given based on their position. Capacity is given based on their inner ability. Train them to be leaders in their own capacity. Unlock and Invest in their potential. Train them to be leaders with good character outside of your circle. Train them to succeed without you. Your team will help you recognize problems you don't see. Teach them how to take ownership that way no is throwing anyone under the bus. Don't limit yourself by using the same team members. Once they've grown, raise the next team. This helps keep fresh eyes.

A few nuggets on leadership

Dominion and leadership

Dominion is about kingdom advancement. When leaders are deployed back into the marketplace (out of the four walls), they must be sent out with a mission to conquer! Why? Because you can't have dominion over something you're not willing to conquer. Dominion is never given to babes. First, you must connect and build relationships with those whom God has assigned to partner with you. Second, you must bring an increase within that assigned circle. Once you've teamed up and brought forth an increase you now must fill the earth (only your place of rule). Filling the earth will help you to subdue (conquer) the adversity in that region.

Timing and leadership

It's very important to understand timing. In this hour when we say dominion, we must think of sons of God.

The more we empower them to think like Christ the more the church will re-establish rule ship. Gods Image- Being made in the image of God means allowing Him to reflect our character to rule. This is how we show the world that God is. 21st-century leaders must understand the timing of God. Now more than ever leaders are being sent into the marketplace to impact the next generation. Discernment on every mountain will give us an advantage over the world because it helps us to see ahead. So, embrace your discernment.

Influence and leadership

Influencing the culture around you (to be leaders) helps you dominate and transform your region. Jesus influenced His followers to do more than Him. He understood that His time upon the earth was limited. Every day people are dying without influencing the world. We have been given a mandate to influence more people and fulfill a greater mandate. So don't limit yourself or your teams.

Responsibility and leadership

Leaders assume responsibility. Authority is tied to responsibility so if you want to lead and walk in authority, you must learn to take responsibility. When you take responsibility, you will have more favor with God and man. You should never think your team is only there to support your vision, but that you learn and bring an increase to each other.

Remember if you stay teachable and always seek to improve you will excel, in your gifts, callings and perfect your ability to lead. Leadership has the power to influence you to become what you think you should become or what others think you should become. *"The most powerful thing a leader can do is believe in your dream enough to teach you how to accomplish it."*

Words to live by

Humble – to be humble means not to be arrogant or prideful. It means you're not partial; you're respectful and don't mind putting other needs before your own. As leaders are evaluated, they must guard their heart. Only your vision and mindset is supposed to shift. However, throughout the years I've seen leaders being evaluated into a position and as soon as they step into position they're heart becomes puffed up, and they lose their ability to see on the level of the people. If your heart is puffed up, you won't be able to understand the needs of the people. Your level of humility should never change because your position changes.

Commitment – making a commitment is being in a state of obligation to connect to someone and something, and maintain that commitment. In 2012 I found myself in a position where I felt like it was time to leave a ministry I grew up in. Although, I knew I was going on to bigger and better things I didn't want to leave because of my commitment to that leadership. Sometimes commitment will have you committed to something for the wrong reason and committed to wrong people.

Integrity - to have integrity means to be honest, connected to moral principles, and having standards. It's keeping your word, yet having the balance, to be honest when you can't.

Respect - respect is an admiration for someone no matter his or her circumstances. Leadership cannot lead effectively without having respect for those who've chosen to follow them. Building strong relationships will allow you to understand them so you can respect them no matter the circumstances.

Listening - when we listen we have to listen with the intent to understand, receive, and interpret all content and every conversation. Without perfecting your ability to listen you cannot properly respond. If you want to follow and run with the vision effectively, you must be able to hear the vision with clarity.

Comprehend – are you able to fully grasp the understanding something because if not you'll never be able to grow your team. The goal of true leadership is to grow people.

Management - the process of steering people in the right direction. No, it's never good to micromanage people, but management is a crucial part of every form of leadership. People need guidance. So don't be afraid to give it.

Apprenticeship

Apprenticeship Instruction Sheet

After completing this book we encourage you to implement an internship to give each participates a chance to put their character, and leadership development to use. Establishing a contract wills ministries and organizations that will allow students to volunteer their time and gift can do this. Doing this, allows you see those who are ready. Just because someone has the knowledge, information and revelation about their assignment doesn't always mean they're ready to interact with people on the next level. Sometimes observing them in action reveals how much responsibility to give them. The internship will give an opportunity for students to use their gift and see how they interact with others. This can bring an increase to your organization, and ministry. It's also important that you placed them with teams, ministries, and organizations they don't know. This will add a little pressure under their feet to see how well they respond to confrontation. Remember character is best displayed when you're in the heat of the moment because it shows others what's on the inside of you.

Building your core components for your Apprenticeship

- The first set up a system of protocol, rules, code of ethics and confidential agreement forms.
- Next, connect with the right ministries/ organizations interested in your volunteer services.
- Interview those interested to get a clear understanding of their ministry and organizational need.
- Then evaluate students, to determine which teams fit them.
- Put together a package for each student that will serve as an evaluation package.
- Suggested time frame would be 30, 60 or 90 days of volunteer work.

Code of conduct

Protocol <u>Webster defines-</u> the official procedure or system of rules governing affairs of state or diplomatic occasions. To establish a code of procedures in a group, organization, or situation.

Protocols are set in place to train, but mainly to help the flow of an organization. Rules help each member to understand how to stay in their own lane. It's not about preventing your team from flowing, but teaching them how to flow in oneness that creates synergy. Throughout many years, I've seen people get wounded because the system of their organization was designed to shut them down. Jesus empowered His team to do greater without Him. The mandate is to rise up leaders to function in their own capacity. So, establishing a system of protocol will only enhance and advance your organization if you let it. People given delegated authority should always serve with intent to do so according to their leader's vision. Protocol helps to stabilize, structure, and again keep a consistent flow. If a leader desires to be effective, they must remember the importance of letting their teams know was required, and make sure they understand all your expectations.

A code of ethics is a document outlining the mission, value of the ministry, organization and how professionals are supposed to approach problems. The ethical principles based on the organization's core values and the standards to which the professional is held.

When an organization assigns leaders to a position without giving them a written code of ethics documentation, they leave the door open for assumption. A code of ethics helps the individuals understand what you expect out of their role as a leader. It stirs up the right behavior and creates a peaceful and rewarding environment.

Dress code: the dress code should be modesty. Which means to dress appropriately as a representative of your team. Considering what look you want to give off for the advancement of your organization. As women, it's important to understand that you are not there to be a stumbling block to anyone with your breast out and clothing that's too revealing. Holiness is a matter of the heart that creates an attitude and produces your outward appearance. This applies to the men also. If your appearance doesn't reflect holiness, it could be a cry for help. Men should have a clean-cut shave, and not have any chest hair showing. Your dress code will always reveal how far you will advance to the next level as a leader. They're some platforms you will never embrace if you're not willing to change. As leaders, it's not about you, but where you're going and the lives you're supposed to impact.

Code of action- your actions consist of your heart, attitude, and your behavior towards others, the company, and self. If your heart isn't right, it can create a negative attitude that affects your behavior. Your behavior helps to shape your character with other. As leaders, it's a must that we stay prayerful and seek help concerning your internal issues. Sometimes, we as leaders may not know of the effects our behavior has on those under our leadership. Those we submit ourselves to can help mature us so we won't offend those who have chosen to follow us. That's important to remember. People choose to follow you!

Any leader that's looking to leave a legacy should include the fruit of the Spirit into their written code of ethics. How well you train your leaders in these areas will determine the longevity of your organization. You can't sell a product without hiring people who are relational and know how to interact with the people with a smile. I've been to ministries and organizations where those in position had a nasty attitude. When a person has a bad attitude, it's hard to believe that they're a believer in what they're selling. Whenever you believe in what you have, you're excited and looking for a way to share it because you want others to enjoy the excitement with you. Even though we're not of this world we still must respect, follow and obey the laws this system has. Although our Christianity may not be respected honored or appreciated, it doesn't give us the right to break them. God grants favor to those who understand the protocol and how any system is running.

When it's time to break protocol, God will let you know. There were so many people in the bible given favor when it was time to break protocol. Because of their obedience to a Godless system when God was ready to shift, he used them. God will break protocol to re-establish order for His people. If Esther had gone before the king in a season without grace and favor upon her, she would have been killed.

Code of order- God is a God of order! He never tells us to forbid others from prophesying, speaking, teaching, or serving in any capacity. He just wants us to establish order so we can bring usher in the flow. When Jesus fed the four and five thousand, He first established a system or order. By the disciples following the system and making the people get in position the increase came and there was an overflow. We must set boundaries when we're building. The goal should be to enhance the performance of your team. Here is a list of why we need order.

- Bring edification
- Bring advancement
- Bring consistency
- Bring protection for the team, not just core leadership.
- Bring protection against confusion and partiality
- Bring effective communication
- Bring understanding for collaborative assigns
- Bring and builds trust for teams to work together

Even when you don't always agree with them, you won't abandon them. Abandon means to give up completely on. The leaders today have become so wounded that their mindsets have become " I'm not Jesus"! If you don't agree with them, they cut you off, and instead of trying to bring freedom and understanding they're praying to bring death and destruction to shut you down. Instead of praying for them to encounter the truth, their praying for the closed door. Until our leaders yield to the mantle of the Shamar, the people will continue to be scattered. When Jesus left, He told Peter not just to feed the sheep, but also to tend to them. Tending to them means to guard and protect (Shamar) them.

We have to nurture them with the word and protect them from every demonic spirit. This requires the activation of their senses. Unfortunately, many leaders' senses today have become dull. We can't teach others how to engage in their assignment until we become their example. Engage mean to captivate and capture the interest of another. When a leader knows how to engage in their assignment not just by nurturing the people but protecting them, it becomes a behavior and a mentality that others will pick up. Keeping them interest or shall I say engage in their assignment can be accomplished through empowerment.

Virtue is empowerment, so don't be afraid to impart into them. Another way to keep them engaged in their assignment is by cultivating their intellect by asking them questions. Questions will let them know how much you value their opinion. It will also keep them communicating, interested and will ignite them to be problem solvers. Next, teaching them the art of focus will build endurance and cancel out distraction. Sometimes, we become frustrated about the process it takes to accomplish a task, and we feel like giving up. But, we must train them to understand the process. The process prepares us to finish the task successfully. Staying focus on the goal will help them get through the process. Remember, you must guard them and be the example. A lot of times leaders start out loving and protecting the people. Hardship and the cares of the world will choke the assignment to love and protect the people out of the leader. Don't allow it!

For best results

Set- up a course outline to help keep students engaged. Following these examples will increase performance and productivity. After carefully reading each section establish an open dialogue for students to discuss everything that was discussed. Do a recap to see if your students are retaining the information. Follow these steps, and examples of homework assignments, for better results.

1. Always stop to explain each section after reading
2. Have each student do a self-examination checklist
3. Open for discussion
4. Have each student research a leader that shaped our country
5. Have the students find the leadership qualities in themselves and list them
6. Have students ask those around them to assess them
7. Instruct them to keep a journal throughout the program and list their emotions and thoughts
8. Encourage them to seek a leadership mentor and accountability

9. Encourage them to list strongest character traits, weakest traits
10. During stage two establish teams and choose a team leader
11. Lastly have each student end with a speech defining themselves, their purpose and their role as a leader

Example: of Self – examination check sheet

Following the sheet students can see what areas they need improvement in. At the end of the program, a review to check should be done to see if there were any improvement.

- ➤ Example (1) do you feel confident when speaking to others
- ➤ Examples (2) name three of your strongest character traits
- ➤ Example (3) list three of your worst character traits
- ➤ Example (4) do you believe you are a leader
- ➤ Example (5) what are your thoughts on leadership
- ➤ Example (6) what are your gifts
- ➤ Example (7) what is your purpose
- ➤ Example (8) do you believe you will ever accomplish them
- ➤ Example (9) list of fears
- ➤ Example (10) what are you willing to change to fulfill your purpose

These are just a few examples to use when creating your self-examination sheets for you, or your students. A survey is also a great way to see what type of classes interest those seeking character building or leadership coaching. This sheet should be kept with you always, to evaluate the behavior, social skills, and any flaws among your class, to help them improve.

Questionnaire

- ➢ Do you always think about getting rid of the competition rather than compete?
- ➢ Do you establish a relationship based on what others have told you about a person?
- ➢ Do you think of winning at any cost?
- ➢ Do you feel like a failure at times?
- ➢ Do you play on others vulnerability?
- ➢ Are you always looking to benefit off others pain?
- ➢ Do you often think you're the greatest at everything, and no one can do it better?
- ➢ Do you judge others based on your personal imperfections?
- ➢ Are you comparing yourself to others?

If you answered yes to these questions, it's time to get healed, delivered and free from insecurities. Until you are free, you won't be effective leading others. Committing to your process will reveal any potential flaws that will hinder you from progressing. Remember you can't empower others until you learn to empower yourself first!

Printed in the United States
By Bookmasters